That Reminds Me of A Story

327 Short Personal Narratives That Inspire You to Collect Your Stories

Wayne Nalls

Copyright Number: 14000350948

Copyright © 2024

All Rights Reserved

Dedication

I dedicate this book of short stories to my wife and companion, who impacted our life journey and raised our two children and me to be good citizens.

Acknowledgment

I'm incredibly grateful to the people who encouraged me to capture the stories in this book before the wonderful memories faded. They supported writing my legacy so family, friends, and later generations could remember me as I was.

Contents

Dedication iii

Acknowledgment iv

Preface xx

Introduction xxii

SECTION 1 - THOSE WERE THE DAYS 1

    Four Lessons Learned from Buying the Second-Best Bicycle ... 2

    Someone Won and Someone Lost, but There Were No Losers . 3

    Forget Expectations 5

    They Are Not Here Anymore 6

    The Old Radio 8

    Vinyl Records 9

    The National Hardware Show 10

    Camp Out 12

    Age Affects Your Concept of Money 13

    I Was Shot 14

    An Old Chair and a Worn-Out Couch 16

    Capture Memories While You Can Still Recall Them 17

A Quick Look Back 19

John Carl's New Boots 20

Jobs That Have Gone Away 21

Bring Your Shoehorn 22

The Secret of the Staple Remover 23

The Children Wanted a Puppy 24

An Apple for the Teacher 26

Trick or Treat 26

Radio was Magical 28

For the Love of Cars 29

The Father and Son Race 30

The Legacy of the Rolling Store 31

SECTION 2 - LIVING LIFE 33

Three Pictures Ten Dollars 34

You Go Before Me 35

A Lesson in Ownership 36

The Three-Way Change of Control 38

Red Hospital Walking Socks 40

Except for the Red Light 41

No Free Meals 43

The Yellow Traffic Light 44

Show an Interest 45

I Wasn't Eavesdropping 46

Stuff 47

People and the Power of Ideas 48

Three Distractions to Personal Success 50

Start, Do, and Complete 51

Accept Yourself 52

The Night I Witnessed a Professional 53

Table Conversation 54

The Bikers Next Door 56

Wise Advice 57

You Should Have Known Carl 57

Things that I Can't Give Away 59

Why People Touch "Wet "Paint" Signs 61

A Dream Deferred 62

Senior Citizens Wit 63

More Than Absentmindedness 64

Mister 64

SECTION 3: THE POWER OF SELF-IMPROVEMENT 66

Why A Short Pencil Is Better Than a Long Memory 67

The Magic Starts with the Dream 68

Learn to Become Better at the Art of Living 69

Be Your Hero 71

What It Takes to be an Achiever 74

Eight Guidelines for Setting Goals 76

Five Ways to Being Your Best 78

When You Win, Everyone Wins 79

The Power of Values 81

Successful People Color Outside the Lines 82

I Will Get That Bone Too 84

Do You Get It Done? 86

For Success, Nothing Beats Preparation 87

Set Goals for Success 89

Self-Discipline Precedes Self-Improvement 91

Seven Reasons Why People Fail to Plan 93

Be A Difference Maker 95

Read Up. Speak Up and Rise Above the Ordinary 97

Think Positive 98

Believe in Yourself 99

Who is On Your Happiness Bus? 100

Tips on Public Speaking 101

Seldom Are We Honest with Ourselves 103

A Professional 105

SECTION 4: THE POWER OF MOTIVATION 107

The Caravan Story 108

The Rope Story 109

Don't Fear Tomorrow. Be Fearful You Will Miss Today 110

First Row a Little Boat 112

The Lazy Man's Way to Riches 114

How to Make Better Decisions 115

Facing Up to Obstacles 117

Before You Say It Cannot Be Done 118

I Haven't Had a Chance 119

Do You Like Britain's Got Talent 120

Eliminate the Participation Trophy 121

Forget the Wake, Steer the Boat, and Keep Your Eyes on the Goal
.... 122

Job Passion 123

Use "And" More Often Than "But" 124

Thirteen Ideas for Success in Any Occupation 126

I Am a Supporter and not a Celebrity. 128

Black and White Hands 129

Instant Charisma 131

Is Your Work Shift Ever Over? 133

SECTION 5: THOUGHTS 135

The Rain Remembers 136

Dictionaries Define Things, or Do They? 136

Possibilities 138

Reset Expectations 139

Make a Difference 140

The Butterfly Effect 142

Whittling 143

Parenting 144

The Buck Stops Here 145

Don't Believe Everything You Read 146

Two Big Fat Lies We Tell Ourselves 148

Where Did the Positive News Go? 149

Teamwork vs. Kamikaze Recklessness 150

Choose the Coach Over the Team 152

The Art of the Handwritten Letter 154

My Name Isn't on A $50 Bill. But It's on My Credit Card 155

Ten Tips for Living a Happy Life from a Backyard Gardner. 157

Fourteen Ideas for Success in Any Occupation 159

Exploring the World Beyond Your Comfort Zone .. 161

Six Thoughts on Success 162

A Steal at a Yard Sale 163

SECTION 6: THE VALUE OF TIME 165

The First Activity of the Day 166

Some Things Are Just Worth the Time 168

How Did it Get So Late So Soon? 170

A Time to Let Go 171

See The End of The Day in The Start of The Day 172

We Know So Little 174

Time Another Success Dimension 175

SECTION 7: FOOD FOR THE SOUL 178

Hoecake and Michelangelo 179

The Disappearing Pie 179

Snickers 181

Peanut Butter 181

Second Chance 183

Defining Moments 183

Oreo Cookies 184

I Smell Ice Cream 185

My Wife's Soup 187

Dinner on the Grounds 187

Today Was a Good Day for a Hamburger 188

The Thanksgiving Meal 190

SECTION 8: PERSONAL STORIES 192

Halt. Who is There? 193

Pennies 194

Twice I Met the Governor 195

Angels in the Neighborhood 196

While I continued to Type 197

Expect Obstacles 198

My First Day on the Job 199

Supporting Role 201

I Like to Remember, But I Don't 201

A Powerful Black and White Teaching Moment 202

Fire in the Dorm 204

What is the Next Million Dollar Idea? 205

Personal Introductions 206

One Sunday and Six Saturdays 208

A Canadian Visit Memory 209

A Senior Moment 210

Rich Man, Poor Boy 210

A Doctor, a Carpenter, and a Realtor 212

Sometimes, Before You Ask, You Know the Answer 213

A Moving Staircase 214

I've Walked This Road Before 215

Sometimes, a Dog is Not Man's Best Friend 217

Yes Ma'am 218

Prince to Pauper 219

Sixth Birthday 220

The Over Night Tan Man 221

Collateral 222

My Favorite Writer 223

The Realtor Who Helped Us in Need 225

Bingo B 22 226

Three Speeches 227

SECTION 9: OBSERVATIONS I'VE MADE 229

Observations from the Sidewalk 230

Our Daughter Needed a Good Samaritan 231

I Am God's Masterpiece 233

I'd Get More Willies 234

Why Is It Difficult to Say "Thank You?" 238

The Master of Truth 240

There Are Well-Mannered People 241

When You Know Little 243

Fingerprints, Snowflakes, and You 244

A Servant Leader is the Phantom that Empowers Others 246

The Not-So-Secret Sabotage 247

One Well-Told Story Packs More Power Than 1,000 Business Cards 249

Put Your Opinions to the Test 250

Setting New Year's Resolutions 252

Guard Against Idea Assassins 254

Aging 256

Where did the U.S.A. Today Go? 257

People Are Different 257

OCD 259

SECTION 10: GROWING UP 261

I Still Have Dreams 262

Looking Back 263

Learning to Drive 265

Growing Up 267

Lessons Learned Early Are Better Than Lessons Learned Late 269

Battle Creek, Michigan 271

The Broken Twig on Mother's Azalea Bush 272

Thomas and His New Glove 273

Killing Without Motive Is Still Murder 275

First Date 276

Two Job Applicants and One Job 277

SECTION 11: STORIES I HAVE READ WHILE SITTING ON MY FRONT PORCH 278

Awareness is a Powerful Word 279

Readers Like Fishermen, Don't Let the Big Ones Get Away. 280

A Person is A Person, No Matter How Small 281

Julius 283

The Greatest Salesman in the World 284

The Magic of Thinking Big 285

Take A Message to Garcia and Get it Done 288

SECTION 12: THE REST OF THE STORIES 290

Courtesy Is the Minimum for Doing Business 291

Work in Progress.. 292

Life Through the Eyes of a Child 293

Keys 294

Passing on Treasures... 295

We Work and Often Forget the Reason for the Work 296

The Nearest Exit May Behind You... 297

Two Perspectives 299

The Obvious Case for a Garage 300

Should Company Restroom Expenses be Included in the Marketing Budget?.. 301

Don't Be Fooled by the Mask... 303

What Has Society Done That David Copperfield Couldn't?.. 305

Don't be Disqualified for the Trophy 307

Maps and Directions 308

Corrugated Cardboard Boxes... 309

SECTION 13: STORIES TO BRIGHTEN YOUR DAY 311

Twinkling of an Eye.. 312

The Salty, Savory Sea	313
A Story of Two Donkeys	314
The Bible's First Ventriloquist	315
I Did Not See That Coming	317
Disciple May Describe It Best	318
The Nursery Mom	319
Don't Look for Level Plains. Climb Mountains	320
When the Gospel Songs Go Silent	321
Journey to the Top	322
A Two-Part Command: Ask and Seek	323
That's Not What We Do Here	324
Diamonds are Forever	325
Kindness	327
Prayer Is Talking with God	328
Zippo Lighter	329
People Can Put You in a Pit	330
Meditation	332
The Blue Cow	333
The Unsung Man of Trust	335

About the Author 337

Preface

When my father-in-law spoke to me, he always began the conservation with, "That reminds me of a story." I never figured out what "that" was.

His stories were captivating, but they were not relatable. His hundreds of stories never mentioned his family—his wife and four daughters—and did not contain motivation or incidents others could connect to in their memories.

Curtis talked about his RAF service, crop dusting, and his time with the Apollo missions at Cape Kennedy. This man still needs to graduate from college. He attended the University of Florida for two months and dropped out. College was boring.

Now that I am writing my memories, I took his storyline "That Reminds Me of a Story" and titled it. These short stories are more than reflections on the past. They are reminders of the remembrances we carry with us in every moment.

These stories will inspire you to reflect on your memories and their influence on your life. They will remind you that no matter where life takes you, your reflections will always be a part of you. Most of all, this book encourages you to write your memories while still remembering them. You will enjoy the process, and so will your family and friends.

Come with me on this journey of memories. "That Reminds Me of a Story" reminds you to cherish and share memories. No matter your age, each event is a story worth telling.

Introduction

Looking back on a beautiful memory is one of the pleasures of life, and this book is full of memorable times.

There are many reasons for writing this book. First, I want to capture my memories before I forget them. Second, I want to leave a copy of the book for my children and their children. Third, I want these short stories to remind us of the experiences, lessons learned, and wisdom gained.

This book will challenge and inspire you to write your stories before you forget them.

That Reminds Me of A Story

SECTION 1 - THOSE WERE THE DAYS

Memorable stories that celebrate the younger days.

Wayne Nalls

Four Lessons Learned from Buying the Second-Best Bicycle

I was ready to buy my Phantom, but the bicycle dealer said they had sold out and only had the Green Hornet in stock. My disappointment showed. But the Hornet wasn't bad either, never mind that it was second best. I gave the clerk a $5.00 bill and agreed to pay $2 every Saturday until I paid off the note. The money came out of my paper route. It seemed I had my first taste of credit, got the bike, and paid two dollars every week forever.

I enjoyed riding the bike as time passed but never loved it. I wanted to own a Phantom, and I settled for a Hornet. I liked the best bike, and I chose the second-best bike because I was unwilling to wait for a new shipment of Phantoms to arrive. The Hornet cost slightly less than the best, but I forgot the savings.

I learned four valuable lessons from buying the second-best bicycle.

Lesson 1. Have patience. If I had waited two weeks for the new shipment, I would have gotten the bike I wanted. Lessons learned.

Lesson 2. When what you want costs a little more, don't settle for a bit of saving. We quickly forget the price. Value has a long shelf life.

Lesson 3. I know, looking back, that the "fastness" or speed of the bike resulted from how much energy I spent peddling. Phantoms and Hornets had a chain-driven sprocket with one speed — no derailleur offering multi gears. I peddled slowly, and I crept. I peddled fast, and my speed increased. The same is true of life.

Lesson 4. Anything worth having is worth working for. Sometimes, I was tired of delivering my newspapers. I had to give the man at Western Auto two dollars.

I am sorry for kids who don't earn money to buy a bicycle today. I am sad for kids who have a bike and don't earn money to pay for it. They won't know the joy of patience and the excitement of paying off a "note."

Unable to connect effort and result, cause and effect, between sweat and reward, they only know getting, never giving. Whenever I feel impatient, as I sometimes do, I remember the words of John Quincy Adams, "Patience and perseverance."

I peddle on.

Someone Won and Someone Lost, but There Were No Losers

When I was a kid, I used to play (shoot) marbles—sometimes for "keeps" and sometimes for "fun." You need not have played marbles or even understood how we played to guess which version my parents preferred me to play.

All the kids in the neighborhood understood the goal of the competition. We played football, baseball, horseshoes, cops, and robbers. But when the game, contest, or event was over, and a winner or winners were declared, we were all best friends and buddies. No one lost, and there were no losers. We just moved on to the next competition.

In 2018, it was a technological world. Kids don't shoot marbles in driveways (dirt is needed for the playing field) or play cops and robbers solving neighborhood "crimes." Today, there is no need for two empty soup cans with a string attached to them to communicate — text or call your friends on your cell.

Time brings change—much of it is beneficial. But not all change is positive. Today, many people have adopted the mantra of only playing for keeps and forgotten how to have fun. Today, we often recognize the winner and classify all the other participants as losers. Somehow, that doesn't sound right. If you win, you win. If you don't win, you lose. You are not a loser, but you failed.

I like the concept of win/win. But, in today's world, there are "winners" and "losers." Someone won the account; someone else didn't; one team scored more points than the other side; someone was valedictorian; another attended summer school; someone got promoted, and some people got overlooked.

That Reminds Me of A Story

Our goal should be to work hard and be competitive. But when we've given our all, and the game is over, we should move on to the next contest.

Forget Expectations

I attended my first professional baseball game 69 years ago. It was a spring training game in Tampa, FL. My dad took my brother and me to see the New York Yankees and whomever they played that day. As a kid, I loved baseball, mostly the Yankees, who dominated the 50s.

We purchased our tickets and excitedly walked up the ramp to enter the stadium, expecting to see the Yankee "GIANTS." Surprise! I noticed they weren't super giants but ordinary men; men with two arms and two hands, two legs with feet, men in pinstriped baseball suits — and they were small. I had a major disappointment in the Bronx Bombers. What I expected to see wasn't what I saw.

I saw Mantle, Rizzuto, Stengel, Berra, and Joe DiMaggio. That day, I saw Mickey Mantle bat from both sides of the plate and do his famous drag bunt, but there were no home runs.

Mel Allen, the Yankees' play-by-play announcer, was set atop a light pole on a small platform no larger than two wooden pallets, broadcasting the game. Allen was one of the most recognizable voices in radio broadcasting. The scene I saw could have been better and different from what I expected.

The goal of expectations is to experience what you expect. I don't recall which team won; I vividly remember hoping to see "giants" and seeing ordinary men playing baseball. Forget expectations. Live now. Nothing happens next. You're already there. As Buddha said, "Be where you are; otherwise, you will miss your life."

They Are Not Here Anymore

I remember my childhood neighborhood. Five wooden houses were on each side of the road, each with two bedrooms and one bath. Unfortunately, there were no attached garages. Several houses, including ours, had front porches with swings. We did not have carpet or tile, only wood floors. The exception was in the kitchen; we had linoleum.

We had electricity and running water, but my parents got our first home phone (dial-up) in 1947; I was seven years old. Our number was 352-629-1715. We were on a "party line," meaning others could pick up their phone and listen to our conversations.

The driveways were dirt, excellent for shooting marbles and looking for doodlebugs. To see a doodlebug, you placed a finger in its hole and sang, "Doodlebug, doodlebug, come out; your house is on fire."

That Reminds Me of A Story

Yards were grass you mowed with a rotary push mower, but there were no power mowers.

Stinging nettles were everywhere, and we knew their sting well from running barefooted through the woods behind our house. I don't know if that plant is still around or has become extinct. No one has mentioned a stinging nettle in the last forty years, but you remember the sharp pain if it stung you.

In the 40s, our neighbors knew us, and we knew them. Any neighborhood parent could discipline you if they catch you doing something wrong. My brother and I agreed we preferred the neighbor's discipline rather than reporting our actions to our parents, and then they disciplined us.

Freedom best describes my neighborhood. We were free to play any game we chose, open to associating with all the neighborhood kids, and accessible to engage in a heated discussion. Then, we could move on to the next activity and expand our area to include the three streets south and the four streets west.

I remember well the neighborhood fish fry. Several dads fished all day, brought their catch home, cleaned them, and deep-fried them in a big black kettle filled with hot grease (from the wood fire beneath it). When someone did the fish, someone would spoon the dough for the hushpuppies. The mothers brought fresh vegetables, pickles, homemade desserts, and tea.

After the blessing, we ate.

I still recall the wood fire, the sound of boiling grease, onions in the hushpuppies, and the taste of deep-fried fish from 70 years ago.

As much as I loved that neighborhood, it has a downside. My grandchildren won't know how to dial phones, shoot marbles, or run barefoot in nettles. The problem is that today's children will not experience a neighborhood fish fry with hushpuppies, pecan pie, and neighbors who love them.

The Old Radio

I'm looking at the old 1940 model S9496809 Zenith radio in my living room. The 80-year journey with this radio brings back memories. The radio has a shortwave band, and I remember listening to the BBC in London, ship-to-ship radio conversations, and the Grand Ole Opry on WSM in Nashville.

My two favorite memories are listening to The Lone Ranger, sponsored by Merita Bread, and sending many logos to Battle Creek, Michigan, for silver bullets, decoder rings, and the famous black mask. Battle Creek was the first out-of-state town I knew.

My second-best memory of listening to the ham radio was the operators' classic call: CQ 20 meters. That meant the caller was attempting to connect with any other ham operator. QSL was a

That Reminds Me of A Story

response from Ham radio operators saying I received the call. QSL is the CB equivalent of Ten-four (10-4).

I wanted to be a ham operator, but I could not distinguish between the dits and the dahs, though I memorized the Morse code. My dream of getting a ham operator's license has yet to happen.

My father surprised the family when, in the late 40s, he bought a small turntable to sit atop the radio and play the recorded music through the radio speakers. I recall the first recorded song I heard, "Cool Water," by the Sons of the Pioneers. I still have that 45rpm record.

The best thing I can say about my antique radio is that I have a cell phone, laptop, digital camera, and a 50-inch HD Television. Still, together, they don't equal the memories of my father's old radio.

Vinyl Records

RCA Victor released vinyl LPs in 1930, and they remain popular today. Today, National Vinyl Record Day is on Aug. 12th; it provides a great way to celebrate the oldies.

My granddaughter Anna recently got an old-fashioned turntable record player. She has always loved music, especially the rock and roll of the 50s. How are today's teenagers associated with music from sixty years ago?

Some music is timeless and embraces people of all ages. The music of Elvis, Little Richard, Johnny Cash, and the Platters speaks to the heart.

While my wife and I went through our things and culled out essential items to downsize, I came across some recordings my granddaughter would want. Besides the previously mentioned records, I have Eddie Arnold and Tennessee Ernie Ford recordings. I don't have any Led Zeppelin, Nirvana, or David Bowie records or CDs.

Anna will cherish the original recordings of the old-time radio shows of Superman, Sky King, Sergeant Preston of Yukon, Red Rider, Little Beaver, Hopalong Cassidy, and The Shadow. These are not CDs but songs and adventure stories recorded on vinyl.

I will only explain carbon paper or rotary phones if you know what vinyl records are.

The National Hardware Show

While attending the National Hardware Show in Chicago, I had two unusual experiences.

I witnessed one of the hotel servers make a smooth move after asking a family of four if they wanted water. The response was "Yes." So, he poured four enormous glasses of water. Then, the server returned to the table with a pitcher of orange juice. He carried

That Reminds Me of A Story

the drink to the young boy's glass and said, "Orange juice?' And as with the water, he filled all four customers' glasses with juice. I knew the water was free, and the juice was $3.50 per glass. This family had spent fifteen dollars before they ordered their breakfast. (Back in 1978)

As I left my table, I wondered if the family would order a second round.

I sat on a bench in front of my hotel, waiting for a ride on the show bus. I was thinking about my early breakfast when a young man sat beside me out of nowhere. He asked, "Want to buy a watch?" Quickly, he pulled up his shirt's left sleeve, and 25 to 30 watches were on his arm.

Before I could say, "No, I don't wish to buy a watch," he showed what he claimed to be a Rolex watch. "Only a thousand dollars, "he said. I had never seen a Rolex," but I knew they were expensive.

In a flash, the seller offered me the watch for $750. Sensing my non-interest, he said, "I'll let you have it for $100. The price had dropped from $1,000 to $100 in less than 20 seconds. But he wasn't through with his pitch." How about $25? I said no, and he hurried to his next target, a man sitting about 15 feet away.

It is essential to understand that the orange juice, while expensive for me, could have been a chump change for the father. The $1,000 "Rolex" watch became $25 and is still not worth the price.

Camp Out

On a spring evening in 1950, my younger brother, another 9-year-old boy, and I camped out while discussing something to do. It would be in the great outdoors—my backyard. The campout was our first. As our neighbor friend Maurice said, "The overnight experience would be exciting."

In the night darkness, we would share ghost stories. Scary stories.

At nightfall, we bedded down using some blankets, built a small campfire, and looked at the setting sun. The dimmer the fire became, the darker the night became. The number and variations of sounds we heard, many of which we had never heard, startled us. With the fading light, objects around us became less clear. Bushes were now wild animals, including bears and werewolves.

As it became darker, we told fewer ghost stories. While the flames of the fire died, our friend's mother called for him to come home. Now, the fearsome three became the frightened two. Soon, the fearless two packed up and went inside. The adventure in the great outdoors was over.

That Reminds Me of A Story

Age Affects Your Concept of Money

When I was eleven years old, in addition to my daily newspaper route, I had a Saturday job at my church. Our church custodian paid me fifty cents per hour to rake leaves and pick up trash for three hours.

I liked the job and the dollar and a-half (no taxes) pay. But I knew the custodian was earning $45 a week. In a few years, the janitor would retire, and I hoped to get his job. In the early 50s, forty-five dollars was a lot for a kid. With that pay, I envisioned being rich, set for life.

Twenty years later, while in Graduate school, I heard Dr. Schwartz, my marketing professor and author of "The Magic of Thinking Big," say, "No one in this class should make less than $100,000 a year." I knew I was in the right class but the wrong job.

Dr. Schwartz would earn over $5,000,000 for his books and speaking engagements. It took me fifty-plus years of hard and intelligent work to approach the magic $100,000 earnings level.

Perspective is essential at all levels of life. I saw $2,340 at ten years old as providing a comfortable lifestyle. At 75 and about to retire, I saw $100,000 as significant. At 84, I sit here writing about money. I realize life isn't about the amount of money I earn. It is about something money can't buy. While many of my wants remain, I have all my needs supplied.

I Was Shot

Looking back, I can scarcely remember a day more frightening than the day somebody shot me. In the late 50s and early 60s, hitchhiking was the transportation for young men, especially for short distances.

My home was 30 miles from the university I attended. Each Friday, I packed my laundry and hitchhiked from Gainesville, FL, to Ocala, FL., to visit my parents, and my mother would wash my clothes. On Sunday morning, I hitchhiked back to the university, carrying my bag of clean clothes.

One Sunday morning, much fog made visibility low. I stood by the highway and watched a few cars pass. Suddenly, the driver slammed on the brakes and backed up. I ran to the car, and the driver asked, "Where are you going?" I replied, "To Gainesville." Hop in; the driver said, "I'm on my way to Alachua." (a few miles north of Gainesville).

As soon as I got into the vehicle, I realized something was off. The car was a two-seat model; the driver wore sunglasses (in the fog), and as he drove, the car weaved back and forth between the two lanes.

That Reminds Me of A Story

"Yep," he said. "I'm a truck driver, and when I reported for work this morning, the boss sent me home saying, 'I was too drunk to drive.'" My problem was obvious: a drunk driver and poor road visibility.

The driver said, "I'm not seeing well this morning, and when you see a gas station selling beer, let me know." I need to get out of this car. After several weaving miles, I saw a store he wanted. But I would not tell him about it if he couldn't see it.

We were almost past the store when he saw it. He braked suddenly, and the car swerved toward the two gas pumps in front of the store, stopping right next to them.

He got out of the car and asked me what kind of beer I wanted. I replied, "None." He went into the store to get his beer. I should have gotten out of the car and run. But I didn't

Suddenly, the driver appeared with two cans of beer and asked me to hold them while he got in. I took the beer, and he drew a pistol, pointed it to my head, and questioned, "How long has it been since you got shot, boy?"

Before losing consciousness, I recall seeing a flash of light and thinking, what would my mother say? I have two cans of beer, about to meet Jesus, and I've had no beer.

When I came to, the drunk shook my head and asked me if I was all right. The "gun" was a cigarette lighter shaped like a pistol. The flash I saw was the flame on the wick of the cigarette lighter.

I exited the car and determined I would travel by other means. After walking a one-half mile, I looked down and discovered I was about to step on a dead rattlesnake. Finally, I hitch a ride with a man driving a hearse. He was on his way to pick up a body. I was thankful the body wasn't in the hearse.

I got to the university but never told my mother the shooting story.

An Old Chair and a Worn-Out Couch

A young couple knocked at my mother's door. They asked about the old chair I had put at the curb. Was it for sale? If so, what was the price? I answered their question and told them it was free; they could have it. The couple thanked me and seemed delighted. They said they had recently rented their first apartment and had no furniture; this would look good in their apartment.

My mother passed away recently, and my wife, brother, sister-in-law, and I cleaned her house. I asked them if they could use the matching sofa. What happened next shocked me. After saying yes, they wanted the couch. The man and woman cried.

Puzzled, I asked if I had offended them. The lady said something beautiful: "No, the chair and couch are the only furniture we have for starting a life together."

I read of the discovery of famous paintings and the finding of enormous amounts of money in a piece of furniture bought at a Salvation Army store. Many of us read or hear stories about people finding treasure in old couches and stuffed behind walls. But few stories are like the beat-up couch and worn chair. There was no money socked away in it either.

I remember thinking, " This is my lucky day to have helped a deserving couple with two worn but free furniture pieces. " The couch and chair represented a start for the couple and a joyous feeling for me.

Capture Memories While You Can Still Recall Them

Today is a productive memory day; I have three thoughts from the past that have bubbled up from 1965. While driving from Atlanta to Tampa, Florida, I stopped to get gas. Service stations provided some service even with the regular gas price of $1.19 a gallon.

Before I got the keys out of the car's ignition, a station employee stood beside the car and said, "Mind opening the hood?" He caught me off guard with his request. I had stopped to get gas. The last time

I looked, the gas cap was on the back right-hand side of my car, not under the hood. So, I pulled the hood release.

I exited the car and came to its front; the employee had this sizeable circular object in his hands and tapped the ground with it. "Mister," he said, "this is costing you money." I did not understand the item he had taken from beneath the hood and was tapping it on the concrete pad. Dust flew everywhere. His next question was, "When did you last change your air filter?" So that's the item in his hand, an air filter.

In eight years of driving, I never changed the air filter in any of my vehicles.

"Can I change this for you? You'll start saving money?" I know nothing about air filters—or any other item under the hood of a car. But I enjoy saving money. "I said sure I'd buy a new one." As he installed the new filter, I told him, "No one has ever mentioned an air filter to me in the eight years I've been driving. So why did you ask me to open the hood, reach in, take the filter out, and tap the filter on the concrete pad so I could see dust and dirt coming out?"

He answered, "Because I get fifty cents for each filter I sell." I said, "I bet you sell many filters." He replied, "I sure do. Every car that stops here is a prospective sale, and I close most of them."

That Reminds Me of A Story

Today, I paid $3.69 for a gallon of gas and pumped it myself. Tomorrow, I must learn how to change my car's air filter.

A Quick Look Back

It would be natural to look ahead and not behind. However, people cannot successfully drive a car, peddle a bicycle, or safely walk if they are always looking back. However, it may help to sneak an occasional backward look to ensure your safety. The past is just that, the past. Former professional baseball pitcher and Hall of Fame Leroy Robert "Satchel" Paige said, "Don't look back—something might be gaining on you."

On a flight out of Tampa, Florida, I listened—a good idea — to the flight attendant's mandatory preflight safety announcements. She addressed seat belts, oxygen masks, no smoking, float devices, service trays, etc. When she talked about exiting the plane, she told us to look for the closest exit sign should an emergency occur. The flight attendant reminded the passengers that the nearest exit might be behind, even in the next row back.

A quick look back helps determine whether you are on target or missing the goal. The scoreboard reveals the winners and the losers. You are achieving your goals, or you are not. Recognize the shortfalls and take corrective action. Tout the achievements and build on the momentum. Look back and verify that the objectives you set in the past are still realistic.

The past is often a burden for the future. Even when executed brilliantly today, a strategy that produced success in the past frequently leads to failure. Blame it on change. Great advertising executive Bruce Barton observed, "When you are through changing, you are through." Look at a caterpillar and look at a butterfly. The only connection is change. As someone said, "If nothing ever changed, there'd be no butterflies."

While what is behind (the past) is essential, it is also necessary to look around (the present). Both the past and the present are often a harbinger of the future. Today, a sensitive appraisal viewed in the past's light can help eliminate repeating historical mistakes.

John Carl's New Boots

His grandmother promised him a pair of cowboy boots, his first. He asked about those boots every few minutes: "When will we get them?" "Where will we go to buy them?" "Isn't it about time to go?"

After a few minutes, the six-year-old child asked his grandmother, "Can we get the boots now?" Grandmother answered, "If you don't quit asking about those boots, I will not buy them for you." There was a five-minute silence, and the child said, "I haven't asked about the boots in a while."

The young boy's trip to the shoe store for cowboy boots was quick, but the transition from wanting boots to swaggering out in them was longer.

The Cowboy Boot Brand—Justin, Corral, or Rocketbuster—wasn't necessary. The transforming element was authentic cowboy boots, and for a moment, the shoes transformed the young boy into John Wayne, Red Rider, and The Lone Ranger. His grandmother started the change; the shoe clerk facilitated the change. Still, the boots changed the young boy's swagger into a self-assured hero, shoulders straight and a clinched face sending the message. I am a cowboy.

Jobs That Have Gone Away

When I was a kid, I had a newspaper route. I earned more than the 40 cents an hour minimum wage. They based my earnings on the number of papers I delivered. It wasn't until eleven years later (1956) that the minimum wage was one dollar an hour.

After school, I rode my bicycle to deliver papers and made rounds on Saturday to collect the money for the provided papers. That was enough money for my Schwinn Green Hornet bicycle and the movie show on Saturday afternoons.

With the arrival of television in the 50s, the decline in newspapers began as the source of most people's news. With less newspaper circulation, there was less need for newspaper delivery. Today, the internet provides people with up-to-date information as it occurs.

I miss the smell and sounds of the printing room, rolling the papers and binding them. I enjoyed throwing the newspapers and meeting my customers on Saturday morning as I collected for the past week's delivery. I was an entrepreneur in those days.

Kids can't do that today—and not just because the newspaper boy jobs are gone—we employ many kids and some adults for an average minimum wage of $12. Manufacturing workers replaced by technology often must search for less-paid jobs.

If you're willing to work hard and go the extra mile, get out of a career that is in decline.

Bring Your Shoehorn

Unlike the other shoe stores I was in this morning, Carnival stocks only shoes, and many of them. When you find a pair of shoes you want to try on and ask for a shoehorn, you don't expect to hear, "We don't have a shoehorn."

I clearly remember when you went to purchase shoes. A salesperson assisted you in finding the right shoes and helped you get them on to ensure you were fit. Today, there are no salespeople, clerks, shoehorns, or salesmen. And with no X-ray, you could put your feet in and look at your feet in the shoes.

It is nice to know that the United States has the most significant footwear market globally, amounting to over 91 billion U.S. dollars in revenue in 2019. Consumers worldwide buy about 14.5 billion to 19 billion pairs of shoes annually.

As of 2021, about 927 shoe and footwear manufacturing businesses are in the U.S. These manufacturers could help by providing their retail customers with shoehorns. Then, when a retail buyer needs to try on a pair of shoes, they would have a shoehorn to help them.

Times have changed. Today's retail shoe industry lacks service or shoehorns and will soon be out of business. Retail shoe stores should post a sign in their windows saying, "Bring your shoehorn."

The Secret of the Staple Remover

It sometimes appears I have seen everything. But catching someone doing a complex task using a hand staple remover reminds me that there are still areas to be discovered.

One day at work, I watched a young intern complete her job assignment, removing staples from a pile of papers and separating them to be shredded. As I observed her, I realized that any simple task could become complicated by untrained people. The intern was misusing her hand stapler remover. Instead of squeezing the jaws to release the used staple, she utilized the prongs to straighten the two backside staples. Then, she flipped the paper again, slid the teeth under the front side of the staple, and removed the staple.

It happens; in the hustle and bustle of work, we accidentally staple unrelated documents and need a tool to fix the error. Presto! It's a simple hand staple remover. A hand staple remover can quickly take out staples without damaging the paper. If misused, you risk ruining your documents with rips—and waste time while looking foolish.

Knowing how to use a staple remover makes it the perfect tool for the job. The question is whether the organization adequately trained employees to do the job.

The Children Wanted a Puppy

There are many things children want, and some of them are expensive. When my wife and I lived in Grand Rapids, Michigan, our two young children decided they wanted a puppy. After repeatedly saying you don't need a puppy, we agreed to take them to a pet store and let them look at the puppies for sale — the operative phrase was "look at." For Natalie and John-Carl, it meant they would get a puppy.

Upon entering the pet store, I immediately experienced puppy

That Reminds Me of A Story

sticker shock. The price of puppies was high, and the puppy my kids singled out, a Siberian husky, was $175. I told the two young mushers we were not buying, raising, or training a husky to run the Iditarod.

There was no way I was paying one hundred and seventy-five dollars for a puppy, even though the Siberian was a beautiful black and white puppy with two blue eyes. While most dogs have brown eyes, many Siberian huskies have striking blue eyes.

I told the kids that if they could find a husky with two blue eyes for under $100, I would buy it. Little did I realize the perseverance of a 10-year-old and a 12-year-old. They searched the newspaper classifieds daily. Then, one day, they surprised me with the exact husky they were looking for and the same price I had willingly agreed to pay.

They found their prized puppy quicker than a college fund-raising committee finds you after moving. They named the dog Major because this was a significant win for them. The young mushers outfoxed their dad.

Maybe it's just me, but if I bought a puppy today, I would visit the local Humane Society.

An Apple for the Teacher

"A good teacher is like a candle — it consumes itself to light the way for others." Mustafa Kemal Atatürk

The important thing in life is not to get additional education but to discover the application for your information. It's impossible to alter what has already taken place. Whatever your age, people have abundant knowledge, information, and wisdom to tap into living a better life.

Self-education involves applying knowledge and experiences to create new ideas. It is nature's way of making new applications to keep you relevant.

Many people need to know to listen carefully to their inner voice. Your inner voice knows you better than anyone based on your values, environment, education, people you hang out with, and life experiences. Prepare for tomorrow by applying your present information.

You are the teacher of life. When you recognize that your inner teacher is the only teacher who matters, give yourself an apple.

Trick or Treat

My memories of Halloween at my church are non-existent. We didn't celebrate it. One senior lady described it as the "works of the devil." We celebrated Christmas, Easter, Thanksgiving, and the Fourth of July.

On the last Saturday in October, all the kids dressed as Batman, Swamp Witch Hattie, the Shadow, or Donald Duck went door to door asking for treats. We enjoyed the neighborhood parents' candy, nickels, and other goodies. Even the local Dairy Queen offered trick-and-treaters a tiny ice cream cone.

When we returned home, we ate candy and more candy. There weren't worries about laced candy or pieces of a razor blade hidden in the candy.

People have stories about their favorite Halloween Trick or Treat evening with ghosts and goblins. It was a frightening time that created scary visions, sounds, and movements that were not there. But our imaginations can affect our emotions.

The holiday was once scary. Now, it is terrifying; some misdirected people poison candy, shootings, and other horrific happenings.

Hold on to your Halloween stories. Your memories are better than today's reality. If you have young children or grandchildren, don't spoil the event's excitement, but be watchful and check all the treats they bring home.

Many treats but no tricks were the results of my evening.

Radio was Magical

My family's first radio was magical. As a kid, I would listen to it for hours. When I turned it on, I heard the William Tell Overture, which introduced the story of The Lone Ranger and Tonto fighting for justice in the West. Dial another station and the Man of Steel, Superman, who came from planet Krypton to save the world. His parents sent him to Earth in a small spaceship as a baby. Thirty minutes later, Batman donned his iconic scalloped cape and pointed cowl and took to the shadowy streets, sky, and rooftops of Gotham City.

The Shadow, Green Hornet, Sargent Preston of the Yukon, and Sky King drew us to the evening radio at 5:00. Homework must be done. At 5:00, we entered the magical and imaginative world of storytelling. Wood being pounded on a hard surface were the thundering hoof beats of the great horse, Silver. Crunched cellophane lit the campfire.

Today, I look back on the stories of these superheroes and find that all of them had a stringent moral code and a strong sense of justice. As a child, life was simpler; right was right, and wrong was wrong. In my childhood, the good guy was good, and the bad guy was terrible.

That Reminds Me of A Story

For the Love of Cars

In the early 60s, introducing new model cars was an event. Local auto dealers revealed the latest models with great fanfare. They covered showrooms with paper, creating a mystique about the design of the new models. It was show time: balloons, popcorn sodas, and pencils. In 1967, the USA had 80 million registered automobiles. Playing calm, I bought one of the 77,976 Ford Thunderbirds produced that year.

I was married for less than two years. One evening, my wife and I were sitting on our tiny apartment porch looking at our dirty Ford car when I said, "There must be an easier way to get a clean car." She jokingly replied, "We can go buy a new car."

The Ford Dealership was only four miles away. We bought a new Thunderbird. We didn't know the color because the sun had set, and the dealership lot wasn't well-lit. After we signed the papers, we drove to a K-Mart store and parked, closely facing the building. Our headlights reflected from the store windows. We bought a green car.

In 1967, we paid around $4,000. Today, the selling price of a non-collection Landau is $48,000. Had we held on to that car and taken good care of it, we would have an old green Thunderbird worth more than our current 2022 car.

The Father and Son Race

Sometimes, you learn a lesson just in time. For example, forty years ago, on the return from the grocery store, my son, daughter, and I got caught up in discussing how fast he could run.

I was forty-one, and he was 11 years old. My son said, "I bet I can outrun you, Dad." The weather outside the car was snowy and miserable. The temperature in Alliance, Ohio, was 29 degrees.

The son challenged the alpha male, and I couldn't let it go unchallenged. I stopped the car, leaving the headlights on, and asked my son to step outside into the blistering weather. We would race about 35 yards and prove who was the fastest. His sister stood at the finishing line and counted from 5 to 1. We set off—a determined young man and his confident father.

We didn't need a way of timing the distance, which was unimportant. The winner was the first to cross the finish line. That was me by one step. Cold and out of breath, I declined a rerun. My shaking legs were no match for my son's youthful legs.

I learned three lessons from running the race.
1. Make sure your assumption that you run faster than your competitor is correct.
2. Avoid rerunning the race. Leave victorious.
3. Even though you win by a slight edge, don't brag about your

victory.

I could have lost by one step, and my legacy would be a forty-one-year-old father beaten in a 35-yard race by his 11-year-old son.

The Legacy of the Rolling Store

Sitting on my grandparents' front porch, I saw the approaching dust cloud signaling the soon-to-arrive rolling store. My grandparents and the other customers could expect the truck to roll up and toot its horn at the same time each week. The store's arrival time was every Wednesday, mid-morning.

The stores serviced regular routes. It was common for people who ran rolling stores to swap out merchandise for common farm goods such as eggs, chickens, pecans, shelled corn, or vegetables, for items like flour, shoes, or chewing tobacco.

Rural American families bought into the rolling store's motto: "We Buy Anything, We Sell Everything." This principle gave my grandparents another example of give and take. If I need what you have, I must give you what you need.

Some people are excellent bargainers. Even when bargaining, they are looking to beat the other person. Be cautious in dealing with unknown people. Be sure you want what they have and what you will exchange.

So, the next time you are in a grocery store, think of the great legacy of the rolling store and its ability to bring sellers and customers together for mutual benefit. B. C. Forbes famously said, "The bargain that yields mutual satisfaction is the only one that is apt to be repeated."

While barter habits may change, give and take is an idea that will never be old-fashioned.

SECTION 2 - LIVING LIFE

Step back and enjoy stories about living a good life.

Wayne Nalls

Three Pictures Ten Dollars

A tall, young U.S. Marine serving in Afghanistan visited a bazaar in Kabul with one of his friends, an Army Major. They came upon an enterprising camel owner who offered people an opportunity to photograph his camel.

This Afghan entrepreneur had a sign that read: "Picture of camel, $5.00 Picture of you with the camel, $5.00 and Picture of you riding the camel, $8.00." These were the posted prices, but everyone knows how business gets done in Afghanistan through bargaining. Published prices are the starting point.

The Marine told the camel owner, "I would like three pictures- one of the camel, one of me with the camel, and one of the camels, my buddy, and me — ten dollars." To which the camel owner replied, "Fifteen dollars."

Again, the Marine held up his ten-dollar bill and repeated his offer. The camel owner countered with, "Thirteen dollars."

They were haggling over ten dollars, not three pictures. For the Marine, the ten dollars were small; for the camel owner, they were big. After several more exchanges, the camel owner, realizing that ten dollars was better than nothing, gave in. The Marine got what he wanted, and the camel owner liked what he got.

Sometimes in life, you are the Marine, and sometimes you are the camel owner. To reach your goal, you need to be steadfast. Other times, you must survey the situation, be flexible, and heed the maxim, "A bird in the hand is better than two in the bush."

You Go Before Me

Children should be seen and not heard, sit in their chairs in a restaurant, and be polite to seniors. However, this is usually not the case today.

I remember the elephant rope story when I observed how young children act toward older adults. Every circus has elephants. No matter that, they also had clowns, tigers, and dancing dogs. But elephants, the largest land mammals, draw the attention of boys and girls. Each elephant has a story to tell. The best story is the elephant rope story.

The story illustrates that when a rope ties a baby elephant to a small stake driven into the ground, it will roam out to the rope's length. The young elephant has not developed its strength and cannot pull up the stake. Later, as the elephant grows, he can easily break free from his rope. So, we condition them to stay within their known boundaries.

I recently entered an elevator with two occupants: an older woman and a 10-year-old boy. As the elevator moved, the youngster asked me, "How are you doing, mister?" I said fine. When the elevator stopped and the doors opened, the youngster and I waited for the woman to exit. Then I motioned for the youngster to leave. He said, "No, mister, you go before me. I will keep the door open."

Adolescents need guidance. They need to be taught manners and reinforced by their actions. Children left to their ways are not likely to change; they'll become adults who go their way the wrong way.

Parents must help their children develop social skills. Children will have manners, bad or good. If they don't learn from us, they will learn from someone else. Set boundaries early. Later, as they mature, they can adjust.

A Lesson in Ownership

Children who love pets—especially cats—teach us powerful life lessons. Here's a lesson in ownership taught to me by the eight-year-old who lives across the street from me. Several years ago, this young girl said: "Mr. Wayne, have you seen the feral cat roaming in our neighborhood?" I replied, "No, I haven't seen the feral cat."

Two days later, she asked me, "Mr. Wayne, have you seen the feral black cat that hides in my shrubs?" I replied, "No, I haven't seen the feral black cat that hides in your shrubbery." I was glad I had asked my wife, "What is a feral cat?" Because her next question was, "Mr.

Wayne, do you know what a feral cat is?" "Yes," I answered, "a wild, homeless cat."

The next day, the young girl said: "Have you seen Shadow?" The feral cat that had become the wild black cat now had a name: Shadow. There is a progression here.

Several days later, as I got into my car, the neighbor girl came running across the street, shouting, "Please, Mr. Wayne, don't back out over, my cat." For her, the feral cat had now become her cat. She had taken ownership.

This story offers a four-step problem-solving procedure.

Problem Stage 1: The issues are vague, random, and often wild (feral) in form. But something is amiss or brewing. Your challenge is to get your hands around these non-defined, frequently unusual occurrences and mold them into a coherent shape. Problems can't stay feral or wild.

Problem Stage 2: Vague issues are described. How will they affect me? Gather your arms around the looming problem. Name it. Make the problem as visible as possible. Then, look for facts. Each additional information fact brings new knowledge. New knowledge leads to better decisions, leading to better problem resolution.

Problem Stage 3: The problem has a name, and the potential payoff is defined. Identify the problem. Pay careful attention. What you name the problem represents what it is and what it is not. The more specifically you state the problem, the quicker you solve it. Often, in describing the problem, you reveal the solution.

Problem Stage 4: You must take ownership to resolve the problem. Take responsibility. Successful people know they have the power—and the responsibility—to fix the issues that confront them. The courage to face and solve problems defines a successful person. Successful people take ownership of a problem.

Any problem that has the power to affect you is a problem that should have your name of ownership attached to it; look at the issue as an opportunity to exhibit your problem-solving skills.

The Three-Way Change of Control

Since 2000, I've carried three black stones in the right front pocket of my pants. Every time I retrieve my car keys, I contact the stones. I call them "Three-way change of control" stones.

Why three stones?

My son served in the Army for 20 years, flying AH-64D Longbow Apache helicopters. These are expensive aircraft, and the two-person flying team risks their lives operating them. The Army's mandatory regulation ensures the two-pilot team knows who will pilot the helicopter. It's called "The three-way change of control."

That Reminds Me of A Story

If the first pilot wants to hand off the piloting to the co-pilot, he says, "Joe, you are in control." Joe responds and states, "I am in control." Then, the first pilot replies, "You are in control." There is no room for doubt, excuse, or error. The two pilots knew who was in control of flying the helicopter. There are two lives and a $45-million attack helicopter involved.

I used this three-way change of control often in my business career. When I assigned a project or task, I always finished with, "Mary, you are in control." Mary responded, "Wayne, I am in control." When I reply, "Mary, you are in control," there's no room for doubt, excuse, or error.

In my will, I will remind my children of the four principles of the stones:

- **Focus On What's Important.** Stay focused on the one main thing that makes a difference.

- **Commit.** There is an order of commitment. Commit to your faith, family, and organization—in that order.

- **Be The Best You Can Be.** Your stone may not be the biggest, brightest, or costliest. But it is perfect for this stone. Don't strive to be the best; don't settle for less than your best.

- **The Stone Is Solid and Permanent, But Nature Can Break It Down.** In life, change and competition work to wear you down.

Continual learning and training protect against weathering.

Two of the stones are the most important thing my son and daughter will inherit. They will get a little money if my wife and I haven't spent it. But money doesn't carry the memories; the stones do. I thought of my two children whenever I held those stones over the past twenty years. They control their lives, showing integrity, business leadership, and love for their families.

Red Hospital Walking Socks

During an unplanned midnight trip to the hospital emergency room, they required my wife to stay 24 hours for observation. She had gotten up, blacked out, and fallen backward during the night, hitting her head on the marble-topped nightstand beside the bed. After a half-dozen tests and seven stitches, they transferred her to a room six hours later.

Many people fall. Every year, 2.5 million elderly injure themselves because of falls and require treatment in emergency rooms. Falls are severe and costly. The direct medical costs for fall injuries are $34 billion adjusted for inflation.

I thought it unusual when a nurse entered my wife's room and replaced her hospital-issued green "walking socks" with red ones. When I questioned the nurse about the change, she said, "The red socks alert all the nurses on the floor that the wearer is prone to fall." The red socks act as a warning sign and alert the nurses to be extra vigilant.

Businesses want to see disenchanted customers, patrons, or clients wear red walking socks to alert them that the company has fallen out of step with them. It's easy for a customer's loyalty to slip on a late shipment, stumble on a product mix-up, or lose balance over what they perceive as lacking attention, resulting in a loss of sales and even switching to a competitor.

Often, customers will not tell you what you are doing wrong, so sales-fall prevention begins with you. Make a habit of looking for red warning signs and take corrective action.

Significant opportunities often disguised themselves as red-socks problems.

Except for the Red Light

Except for the red light, I was on time for my eye appointment.

The trip began with three consecutive green lights; I was on schedule, and then the red light. As I waited for the light to turn green, several cars on the intersecting road on my right were turning right and pulling ahead. If this light had been green and not red, I would be ahead of them and on time for my appointment.

The light turned green, and I stepped on the gas. Three blocks later, I saw a two-car fender bender in the right lane. It had just happened. If not for the red light, I could have been in one car in the accident. While the timing of events may seem random, they can be more organized than we think.

The book of Ruth opens with a critical event: a famine in Bethlehem in Judah caused Naomi, her husband, Elimelech, and their two sons to move to Moab, where there was food. The sons married local women (Ruth and Orpah). Life was better, but Eli and the two sons soon died, leaving Naomi a widow with two daughters-in-law.

Hearing the famine had ended in Bethlehem in Judah, Naomi and Ruth left and returned to Naomi's homeland. Ruth meets Boaz, and they marry. The book of Ruth has the rest of the story.

By marrying Boaz, Ruth becomes an ancestor of Jesus Christ.

Randomness is not God's method of operating. He has a linear cause-and-effect plan for people's lives. Scripture says, "Believe in the Lord Jesus Christ (cause) and be saved (results)." Humankind devises his randomness plan. God declares, "I have a plan for you." We reply, "I have my plan."

When you arise in the morning, do you take a moment to thank God for the opportunity to live a new day? That "red-light" moment can influence the events to come.

That Reminds Me of A Story

No Free Meals

I stood by the food counter in a local cafeteria during my lunch hour. I noticed a young father at the counter. He had three small children in tow and asked them what they wanted to eat. The youngest child, about four or five years old and so short she could not see the food display, questioned, "Do we get something free?" "No," the father said. "I have already paid for it."

Hope as we may, we cannot get "something for nothing." Even though something appears as "free," people have discovered there is always a cost. There is never something for nothing. To get, we must give.

Sometimes, we give money, exchange our talents, and occasionally, exchange knowledge. We provide our time to get what we want.

People say, "I wish I had the time to do that." Or, "I wish I had more time to get an education or an advanced degree, read a book, travel, exercise, etc." Each time I hear this, I am reminded that we all have the same time.

People's race, education, age, nationality, or economic position cannot extend, bend, buy, barter, or create time. Time is time. How we prioritize our time is the differentiator. People can make time to do what they want to do.

It is not the time but the prioritization that is important. Author

Harvey Mackay said, "Time is free but priceless. You cannot own it, but you can use it. You cannot keep it, but you can spend it. Once you've lost it, you can never get it back."

The Yellow Traffic Light

When I hurry, all the traffic lights between me and my destination display red; if there is no rush, I seem to hit green lights. I know to stop on red and go on green. I also understand that when the light is yellow, and I race my engine to get through the light, a police officer with a traffic citation lurks.

To avoid these points, I have attended a traffic school. I pay enough for car insurance. I don't know if people learn to be better drivers by participating in the half-day session.

I don't remember the stopping distances for cars at different speeds, nor do I recall all the road signs signify. But my time and dollar investment taught me not to race through yellow lights.

Caution is a warning to slow down and stop. Do not speed up, and hope you beat the red light. Sometimes, we need to slow down and heed the yellow light. Caution is sometimes a prudent decision. We make the right decision if we check for facts, seek advice, and weigh our options. With a sense of urgency, we step on the gas and complete a project or decide quickly.

That Reminds Me of A Story

I've witnessed drivers upset when stopped at a red traffic light. A few drivers even talk to the light as if that would change the situation. This inconvenience and delay have the power to turn into road rage. The wise person takes a deep breath, flushes out the anger in their mind, and waits patiently, knowing the light will change.

Show an Interest

When you realize you will never fit into some of your clothes again, it's time to pass them on. Today, my wife carried two large clothing containers to the thrift center at The Florida Baptist Children's Home. These containers held many nice shirts, pants, dresses, and blouses we no longer wore; we had outgrown the clothing.

We used to say, "Someday, we will lose weight and fit into the clothes again." That day hasn't happened and will never occur, so we boxed up the clothes and took them to the Florida Baptist Children's Home.

Upon arrival, a teenage boy carried the two boxes into the receiving room. He noticed two small Miracle Grow bags in my SUV and said, "Planning on planting a garden?" "No, I responded, I'm using it for my flowers." His next question was, "What flowers are you growing?" I replied, "All kinds of flowers." He approached the building's entrance door and said, "Good luck with your garden."

The young man saw two small fertilizer bags, asked two questions, and made one statement based on his observations. It was refreshing to deal with someone interested in me and what I was doing. When was the last time someone showed an interest in you? Or when was the last time you indicated an interest in someone else?

As I grow older, I listen more to what people say, but I am even more mindful of what they do.

I Wasn't Eavesdropping

I wasn't eavesdropping, but I overheard an excellent story about the surprise when a couple's dog died and the happiness they experienced because one company went the extra mile to make a customer happy.

The story was about a couple who had to put their dog down before Christmas. Sad as they were, they also needed clarification about what to do with the large shipment of dog food that Chewy Dog Supply had just delivered.

They called the Chewy hotline, explained their situation, and asked if they could return their recent order for credit. The company's response was, "We will credit your account. Please give your order to a local pet shelter or someone who can use it. We are sorry about your dog's death."

That Reminds Me of A Story

Chewy's goal is to deliver the best products with the best service. The surprise of this story came next. Two days later, the couple received a UPS package from Chewy. Inside was a condolence care regarding their pet's passing and a vase containing a dozen red roses.

The Chewy web page claims, "Happy customers are always our #1 priority, and our team members are passionate about finding new ways to wow pet owners and the industry at large." You didn't ask, but I believe a condolence card and a dozen red roses say, "WOW!"

Stuff

My son was right. "Order a trash dumpster and get it done."

The fifty-four years of marriage collectibles are not another person's treasure. Your family and friends don't appreciate your books, magazines, Christmas decorations, or anything of value. Today, people prefer a simpler life with less stuff.

My stuff — old baseballs, gloves, bats, horseshoes, treasured rocks, ball caps, a collection of figurine pigs — must go to the county trash landfill via a Dempsey Dumpster. Pairing down your treasure can be challenging, so start today.

I'm still figuring out the future, but it won't involve hoarding stuff that is no longer important. My goal is to have fewer possessions and live a lot longer.

People and the Power of Ideas

In 1901, Charles Duell, commissioner of the U.S. Patent Office and Trademark Office, suggested abolishing the office: someone had invented everything. Had his suggestion been accepted, there would not be patent numbers for televisions, DVDs, video games, computers, digital cameras, cell phones, or GPS locators.

The marketplace is transforming. New products, services, technologies, and competitors enter the market daily. Organizations must search for new and better ways to get the job done to succeed today. This search must involve the organization's greatest asset, its people.

Innovative organizations seek to tap their employees' or members' unused creative potential. They create and maintain a climate of recognition and reward for employees. These creative-orientated organizations also allow the leadership to see that innovative behavior becomes usable daily.

Ah hah, moments are elusive. They have wings and take flight, leaving no footprints. It would help if you captured ideas. It would help if you had a few things to grab and hold ideas that bubble up. A pen or pencil, a piece of paper, or an index card are excellent starters. If you are into computers, you need a file labeled "Ideas and Thoughts."

Keep a pad and pen beside your bed on the nightstand so that you can capture the revelations for future study and analysis when the muse befriends you. One idea popped into my head during the night, and I said, "I won't forget that." But the following day, try as I may, the idea is gone.

Creative programs generate many possibilities and increase the chance of having a significant idea. Ideas spawn other thoughts, and these added ideas create new opportunities. Unrelated, even implausible ideas often lead to practical, creative ones.

You are using creative thinking to solve problems, which aids in searching for solutions that are not always obvious. Look for possibilities and what needs to be clarified, at least on the surface. Often, there are better solutions than an obvious answer. So, don't discard your first thoughts; save them until you have exhausted other possibilities. Then, sift through your list of ideas, looking for the one that offers the best potential. As you cull your thoughts, keep in mind Charles F. Kettering's advice, "The typical eye sees the 10 percent bad of an idea and overlooks the 90 percent good."

William H. Swanson, Chairman and CEO of Raytheon, wrote, "Look for what is missing. Many know how to improve what's there; few can see what's not." He says, "Always think about what's missing; what you will find is amazing."

Wayne Nalls

Three Distractions to Personal Success

Distractions clamor for your attention the moment you decide to improve your status. Chief among these distractions is inertia, which the dictionary defines as an indisposition to motion. By avoiding new situations and challenges, we attempt to protect ourselves by staying put and allowing things to remain as they are. Inertia keeps us in our familiar comfort zone but also prevents us from growing and having new and mind-expanding experiences.

The second distraction in your quest for success is the harmful advice of others. Realize that not everyone will be happy if you succeed. Even well-meaning family and friends can be guilty of discouraging comments. While not given from jealousy or envy, these comments are harmful and can dampen your enthusiasm.

Keep your goals and plans to yourself, or only share them with trusted people.

The third distraction is the subtlest: a personal assessment of unworthiness. This often-overlooked distraction, or self-defeating belief, suggests that the goal is too big and you are not good enough. You wrongly assume that you don't have the ability, training, or knowledge to accomplish your goal. The negative voice inside says, "Who are you to expect to achieve this goal?"

Experts say we would only have the goal if it were within our ability to achieve it. Napoleon Hill was on target when he stated, "What the mind of man can conceive and believe it can achieve."

To eliminate distractions, you must move toward your goal, away from negative people, and raise your self-esteem.

Successful people do not let distractions sidetrack them from achieving their goals. They seek the counsel of trusted friends and knowledgeable people to overcome inertia. Winners replace the feeling of unworthiness with thankfulness for their strengths, talents, and abilities.

Start, Do, and Complete

William H. Swanson, when he was the chairman and CEO of Raytheon, warned against being known as a good starter but a poor finisher. There is often tremendous excitement when starting something new. It is essential to maintain that passion throughout the project, especially when difficulties arise or the project encounters negative thinkers or those who lack the commitment to preserve.

Speaking of the importance of maintaining passion through the course of a project, Jesus said, "For which of you, wanting to build a tower, doesn't first sit down and calculate the cost to see if he has enough to complete it? Otherwise after he has laid the foundation and cannot finish it," all the onlookers will make fun of him, saying,

"This man started to build and wasn't able to finish." (Luke 14:28-30, HCSB.)

Most people begin a task with enthusiasm because something new attracts them. But when they meet obstacles, their passion quickly vanishes. Faced with resistance, they threw in the towel. Do you complete what you start?

"Swanson's Rules of Management" and Jesus' teachings in the Bible support the idea of starting, doing, and completing. A great start does not guarantee an excellent finish, but a poor start assures poor results.

Accept Yourself

Build a strong relationship with yourself before building relationships with others. Self-esteem is important.

How can we cultivate a positive relationship with ourselves? Here are four practical guidelines for creating a better self-image: self-image.

- Accept yourself. Accepting yourself begins with the thought that you are unique, unlike any other person. No two people are precisely alike, like fingerprints or snowflakes—you do not have an "identical" twin. You are unique.

That Reminds Me of A Story

- Often, we prioritize or judge people, including ourselves, according to a counterfeit status code. Guidelines could include wealth, power, etc.

- Appreciate yourself. People appreciate themselves in direct proportion to their self-esteem. So, self-esteem is how much you value yourself. My experience is that others will value you no higher than you value yourself; what you see in others is what you see in yourself. If you like yourself, you will like others. If you dislike yourself, you will have a dislike for others.

- Be aware of your potential. Focus on what you can do, not what you cannot do—know your potential and develop your strengths.

- Acknowledge success. Everyone has experienced success in some form, some more than others. Often, people will downplay their achievements or credit them to luck because they lack self-esteem.

The Night I Witnessed a Professional

I've attended two concerts — a Barbara Mandrell show and a Willie Nelson show. That was until a friend gave me two $75 tickets to a Frank Sinatra concert in Cleveland, Ohio. Though I was not a fan of Sinatra or his music, a couple of free $75-dollar tickets to any show in 1990 provided an elaborate night out for my wife and me.

It was a ninety-minute show, and for ninety minutes, Mr. Sinatra commanded the stage and owned the audience, especially the woman sitting next to my wife and me. Throughout his show," including "New York, New York," "Fly Me to the Moon," and "It Was A Very Good Year," the middle-aged lady kept repeatedly repeating, "Frank, I love you, Frank, I love you."

Her first, "Frank, I Love You," began with the opening song and ended with his closing song, "I Have a Crush on You." This fan had a crush on Mr. Sinatra, the perfect professional.

It will never happen, but entertainment would be far better if entertainers focused less on theatrics and more on professionalism. At least we'd understand the words of the songs and make it easier to watch them.

Table Conversation

I have learned a few lessons from downsizing and moving into a Senior Living facility. The amenities are good, except for the smaller living space and the lack of my wife's home cooking.

Social life here centers on the dining room, where most residents eat and gossip. Before entering the group dining room, I saw the

That Reminds Me of A Story

fourteen walkers lined up alongside the hall wall. Fourteen older adults who live in the facilities leave these walkers there.

The facility houses 66 older adults with unique stories, experiences, and dogmatic opinions. Much of the talk needs more support.

The most common word I hear is "Huh." Someone starts a conversation, and immediately, another person asks, Huh? Someone does not tune them in correctly. No one cares; individuals wait to tell their stories. Individuals repeat the stories frequently. But that's no problem; many people have forgotten the story even if somebody said it five minutes ago.

The conversational phrases include: "Didn't we have chicken yesterday?" "I don't like this meatloaf; another person responds, "This is excellent." Several times, I have heard a resident tell her server, "I didn't order that." She did order that but forgot her order between ordering and being served.

Even though there is an open-seating policy, I often get that stare that communicates, "You are in my chair." Two elevators serve our four-floor building. Yesterday, one resident told another not to get in my elevator.

My daily goal is to not sit in someone's seat or take the wrong elevator.

The Bikers Next Door

The sales of motorcycles continued to decline for the first nine months of 2022. Sales have been 384,997, down 5.6% because of the chain of supply problems and the increased production costs for components.

As I ride down the road, I am amazed that many Florida motorcyclists don't wear safety helmets. The state does not have a helmet law. Maybe these bikers believe they are less accident-prone than cyclists in other states.

When my wife and I were first married, we lived in a small duplex with duplexes on both sides. Though the rental company didn't mark the parking spaces, each resident had one.

One evening, my wife and I were ready for an evening out. I found our parking space blocked by three cycles. I went to the neighbor's duplex and politely asked him to remove the scooters. His indigent answer was, "Scooters? Those are Hogs, not scooters"—my faux pas. But three Harley bikers came out and moved their "hogs."

Hog riders say life is more fun when you are on a hog. It's OK to prefer riding on two wheels with or without a helmet. I enjoy riding in my four-wheel car with a roof over my head.

That Reminds Me of A Story

Wise Advice

After working at Goodrich in retail advertising, I accepted an offer to be another company's vice president of advertising.

I was reluctant to tell my manager, the director of marketing, that I was leaving because of our excellent relationship, but I made an appointment to see him. After entering his office and telling him why I was there, I was surprised when he said, "Congratulations on the promotion. I know you will continue to do the excellent work you did here."

His professional gesture did not surprise me. But it shocked me at the wise advice he gave me. "When you get to your new job, change nothing immediately. If they are profitable, they must do something right. Evaluate what the company is doing right, then humbly improve those actions before making new initiatives."

As I left his office, his last remark was to remember his advice, see what was happening and what was not, listen to trusted counsel, and evaluate your options before deciding.

You Should Have Known Carl

Carl grew up on a farm in South Georgia during the Depression. Sometimes, the crops produced, and occasionally, they didn't. His father could not afford the fertilizer price, so they plowed, planted, and prayed that God would send the needed rain. He had five brothers and one sister. His youngest brother said, "Carl couldn't wait to get off the farm." So, Carl joined the Army. Later, he served in the Marines.

Carl worked at a meatpacking company inspecting for the government. He would faint at the sight of human blood but had no problem performing in an environment spattered with slaughtered cow blood.

People who knew him said Carl's legacy centered on his family and church. He loved his wife and two boys and disciplined the sons. Carl loved football and was a Georgia Bulldogs fan until his sons went to the University of Florida, where he became a Gator fan.

In May 1947, Carl took his family to eat at Bennett's drugstore for Mother's Day. The boys were excited, and when the check came, they asked, "How much did the dinner cost?" Carl said, "Calm down, you two; you act like you've never eaten out." His wife quietly replied, "The boys haven't."

Carl was "right on" when he said, "There are two kinds of people—saved people and people yet to be saved." Carl walked his talk. He took his family to church on Sunday mornings and nights, Wednesday prayer meetings, and 14 nights during a revival. Carl was a deacon, Sunday school, and Training Union teacher and sang in the choir (sometimes he directed the choir). He served as a layman preacher throughout the county.

One Sunday, he preached in a small church, and the chairman of the deacons invited Carl's family to eat dinner with them. The family looked forward to fried chicken. The deacon neglected to inform his wife of the invitation, so Carl and his family went to their house and waited as his wife cooked cans of soup.

His most used phrase was, "God knows." Carl never cursed and used this phrase when he hit his thumb with a hammer. Tools of any type were not his friend.

Carl was a health nut. He lifted weights daily, ate the proper food, never drank, and died of cancer.

Carl was my father.

Things that I Can't Give Away

My wife and I are downsizing and trying to eliminate 55 years of stuff we've accumulated. Before starting, we asked our son and daughter what they wanted of our collectibles. Our son said, "Nothing." Our daughter claimed three or four of our heirlooms.

What do we do with the other 5,000 items?

We've had several yard sales and thrown out a combined 1,000 items. What do we do with the remaining 4,000 items?

Currently, the buzzword in selling is "buy one, get one free." The keyword is FREE! What is better than buying one, get one? I cut to the chase and offered all the items for free. After placing 150+ items at the end of my driveway, I put a Yard Sale sign at my subdivision entry. I added a large, printed sign beneath it that read, " ALL ITEMS ARE FREE."

I sat down on my front porch to see what would happen.

In the next 50 minutes, my sale caused a traffic jam. There were big and small cars, even a Corvette. Trucks of all sizes and a motor home stopped by.

I made several observations:

1. The magic word is FREE.

2. One person's trash is someone's treasure. I observed an individual pick it up only to lay it down. Immediately, someone else grabs the rejected item.

3. Some people will take everything they can fit into their vehicle.

4. If I had to choose between accumulating and eliminating, I would prefer to collect less and eliminate more.

That Reminds Me of A Story

Why People Touch "Wet "Paint" Signs

I often find people touching a wall or piece of woodwork with a sign saying, "Wet paint"? Sure, they can read. But deep down in every one of us is an insatiable desire for proof. We want evidence so much that we touch the paint to satisfy ourselves that it is wet.

Businesses capitalize on this "wet paint" psychology in their industry. If you sell products like brushes or perfume, you can get your customers to touch, feel, smell, or hold your product. The quickest way to do this is to touch, feel, smell, or hold the product yourself first. Then, hand it to the customer and watch him do the same thing!

These are examples of the old art of teaching through imitation. Parents prepare their children by doing the thing to show them how to do it. The children then do the same thing, imitating the parents.

As we grow older, we develop this instinct of imitation. We watch a man swing a golf club, and we can't wait to get our hands on one; a woman sees another woman knitting and immediately wants to hold the needles herself. This action exemplifies the "Monkey see, monkey do" — an act of imitation. And it's a learning process we all engage in.

In your daily life, are your actions and speech worthy of imitation?

Wayne Nalls

A Dream Deferred

A dream can be wonderful when it contains excellent and vivid memories. While I sleep, some dreams make me happy, sad, or frightened.

Dream analysts say nighttime dreams represent our hidden desires and our deepest fears. It's a type of thinking that happens as you sleep.

What we think about at night affects our success and well-being. While dreams are stories and images, they represent information the mind is trying to process to make sense of them.

Our daytime dreams represent the thinking we do during our waking hours. These dreams mean what we feel or want in the future. Our minds create daytime dreams that form images of current and future desires.

You often hear the term "in the zone"—the tendency of certain people to win time after time. Their dream focuses on doing their best and expecting to succeed, which leads to their success.

Like Walt Disney's dream, many daydreams, when acted on, produce happy endings. Like Thomas Edison's dreams, others may not lead to immediate success but take time to light up.

That Reminds Me of A Story

Senior Citizens Wit

Ah, older adults, the unsung heroes of the comical world!

While at the doctor's office recently, I overheard a fascinating conversation. An older lady came to the check-in desk. The nurse asked for a home street address. The patient gave her driver's license and said, "My address is on the license. When anyone wants to know where I live, I give them my license and say, 'It is here on my driving permit.'"

If she became lost while driving, she would approach another person, show them her driver's license, and ask, "How do I get home?"

The next time you see an older adult, watch and listen because it's not age; it's wisdom gained from years of trial and error. It helps to remember that to be old and wise, you must first be young and stupid. My favorite quote on life and aging is from Forest Gump: "Life is like a box of chocolates. You never know what you're gonna get."

While we can't all be Tim Conway or Jackie Gleason, sharing our charm and wit, we can share our laughter and joy.

More Than Absentmindedness

Many people worry about losing things.

I don't know where my things go. I lost my car keys, house keys, eyeglasses, shoehorn, walking cane, and passwords. I quickly forget the location of items, facts, or events.

As I age, the most troubling is my power to concentrate. I think about something and lose the thought while attempting to write it down.

Seeing my beautiful wife is beneficial; I instantly remember her name. If I don't, I need to seek help.

Mister

When my wife and I were first married, like most young couples, we worked and earned less than $125 a week. Love does magic with a weekly income. Mixed with twinkling dust, hard work, and discipline, the amount you have adds up to a happily married 57 years.

We had one car, and my wife dropped me off for work and then drove to her job. She then picked me up after work.

On Friday, during rush hour in Atlanta, I waited for her to pick me up after work. Standing at the busy Five Points Intersection, I knew

That Reminds Me of A Story

that with all the traffic, she would be late. The five-direction lights changed several times in a short period.

Suddenly, a small boy asked me, "Mister, when can we go?" When the red light signaled it was okay to cross, I said, "You can go now." Minutes later, I was asked the same question; the boy had not moved. Again, when our red light came on, I said, "You can go now."

Experiencing traffic fright, the young boy said, "Mister, I am not going till you do."

SECTION 3: THE POWER OF SELF-IMPROVEMENT

Stories to improve self-esteem and increase enthusiasm.

That Reminds Me of A Story

Why A Short Pencil Is Better Than a Long Memory

There is disagreement about how much knowledge we retain in training sessions, but we must remember a large chunk quickly. These training programs offer ideas and strategies for success. People who attend these meetings need to realize the power of pen and note-taking. If I don't take notes, I am not as attentive and focused as I should be.

I can increase my retention level significantly by using a pen or pencil. Note-taking is a sure way to improve retention levels. As someone has said, "A short pencil is better than a long memory."

A person who takes notes listens attentively to what is being said or discussed. Note-taking produces something that is seen and read later. In taking notes, the writer takes part in the learning process.

The benefits of notetaking.

Putting notes down on paper (or computer) gets them out of your head and into concrete form. Ideas are fleeting things. Write them down, and when you review them, they may lead to even more ideas. You collect the information in real time and can process it later. It is easier to reread than to remember. Taking notes forces you to read and listen carefully. When reviewing, notes help you recall the essential things. Reducing ideas and facts to brief notes increases understanding and retention.

A good rule is to write thoughts down when you hear them or when an idea comes to you. Refrain from depending on your memory. Write pertinent information, but don't overwrite it. Use short sentences, fragments of sentences, phrases, and keywords. Focus on salient points.

Taking notes at a seminar or Bible Study can help break the passive role of an attendee, and acting on the messages can increase retention. Don't forget, write it down.

The Magic Starts with the Dream

There was a time that predates Harry Potter, an era of kings, knights, wizards, and magical swords. If you set out to define a magic time in a kid's life, it could be the 6th century — the time of King Arthur and the Knights of the Round Table.

Sometimes, kids played the British king's role, who defeated the Saxons with his legendary magical sword, Excalibur. I was invincible with my magical Excalibur and lived to slay thousands of enemy soldiers and hundreds of fire-breathing dragons. People continue to search for an Excalibur—a magic strategy sword to defeat the "Failure Dragon" and his two bodyguards: Yesterday and Tomorrow.

One fact is that we spend too much time regretting the past and fearing the future. However, regret and fear are not the ingredients of magic. Magic results from a dream fighting for authenticity. Armed with his Excalibur, a contemporary knight can slay the problem.

Humanity has searched for an Excalibur that would turn their dreams into reality. From the beginning, humankind feared darkness. Thomas Edison's Excalibur was the light bulb that transformed the night into day. Mahatma Gandhi used his Excalibur to promote peace and practical, nonviolent actions. Confronting humanity's dream to fly, Orville and Wilbur Wright used their Excalibur to turn it into reality. Louis Pasteur, Dr. William Reed, and Dr. Jonas Salk used their Excalibur to conquer Smallpox, Malaria, and Polio.

We invented the wheel and the printing press with Excalibur to fight immobility and ignorance. Excalibur, Alexander Bell, Helen Keller, Mother Teresa, Newton, Einstein, and Archimedes created magic.

Learn to Become Better at the Art of Living

One way to stretch your mind is through reading. Books lay the world of knowledge at the reader's feet. There are books not worth reading, and some are easier to read and understand than others.

People understood these historical writings quickly when they wrote them, but today, they are hard to master. Shakespeare's poems are difficult for most of us to read and understand. I never understood Old English or the battle between Beowulf and Grendel. But then, I am the one on trial, not Beowulf.

Some months ago, I came across "The Art of Living" (A New Interpretation by Sharon Lebell). The book reveals the wisdom and sayings of Epictetus, a Greek Stoic philosopher (A.D. 55–A.D. 135). Epictetus promoted these thoughts:

- "See things for what they are. When something happens, the only thing within your power is your attitude toward it; you can either accept it or resent it. Things and people are not what we wish them to be or what they seem to be. They are what they are."

- "Events don't hurt us, but our views can. It is our attitude and reactions that give us trouble. We cannot choose our external circumstances, but we can always choose how we respond to them. Discriminate between the events and your interpretation."

- "Avoid adopting other people's negative views. Other people's views and troubles can be contagious. Don't sabotage yourself by adopting negative, unproductive attitudes through your associations with others." Avoid negative thinking of individuals.

- "All advantages have their price. You will never earn the same rewards as others without employing the same methods and investment of time as they do." (Compare to The Law of Causality and The Law of Cause and Effect.

- "Stay the course, in pleasant weather and bad. Regardless of what is going on around you, make the best of what is in your power. And take the rest as it occurs."

- "Corresponding actions preserved and increased every habit and faculty. The habit of walking makes us better walkers." The habit of praying makes us better prayers. Reading pushes us to be better readers. Good habits are hard to break, and so are bad ones.

By expanding our understanding of the world, we grow.

Be Your Hero

"The ordinary man is involved in the action. The hero acts. An immense difference." — Henry Miller

I enjoyed many things growing up in Central Florida, including reading and trading comic books. A comic book costs a dime but delivers a million dollars of high adventure and escapism.

All the kids read and trade comics. Trading two or three comic books could get you one Lone Ranger, Batman, or Superman book. These heroes had extra value, even if only in our minds.

These heroes' books have come a long way. I read a copy of the first comic book featuring Superman, a 1938 edition of Action Comics No. 1, which sold for $1 million at auction. I wish I had known about economics back then. Invest a dime, and eighty years later, trade it for a million dollars. Heck, why not invest in two copies?

People often associate the term hero with sports figures, movie stars, political leaders, and comic book characters. They think of these people as having divine strength, talent, and the ability to defy gravity, stay ageless, or be bulletproof.

Most of us have never considered ourselves heroes. We often view our abilities, talents, and strengths as flaws, failings, and weaknesses. Instead of always wishing we were someone else, we should realize it's okay to be "me."

Some people overestimate their abilities and self-importance. But it has been my experience that more people sell themselves short. The people I meet do not consider themselves heroes. But anyone in any role who performs their best is a hero.

The only way to be a hero is to become more of yourself.

It is impossible to agree on who is a hero, but some situations can develop where a person ceases to be a hero. You stop being a hero

That Reminds Me of A Story

when you:

- Stop learning.
- Stop caring.
- Stop short of the goal.
- Stop being a team player.
- Stop innovating.
- Stop living your core values.
- Stop raising the bar.
- Stop having a positive attitude.
- Stop adding value.
- Stop holding yourself accountable.
- Stop pursuing excellence.
- Stop being the master of your time.
- Stop taking care of your health.
- Stop being an aggressive listener.
- Stop having a sense of humor.
- Stop following up.

- Stop being able to say, "I was wrong."

- Stop leading by example.

- Stop believing in yourself.

Ignore the call to the good and embrace heroism. If you get used to being a hero, you'll be faster than a speeding bullet, more powerful than a locomotive, and able to leap tall buildings in a single bound. Like you, heroes have powers and abilities far beyond those of mortal competitors.

A fictional hero is worth a million dollars. As your hero, what are you worth?

What It Takes to be an Achiever

A young man once dreamed of becoming a Taoist monk and martial arts expert. He visited one of the most influential Masters, Chen Ka Ming. Everyone knew the Master for his martial arts skills and philosophy of life.

As the young man entered the Monastery, Master Chen Ka Ming invited him and asked him why he wanted to become a Taoist monk. Surprised, the Master knew his reason for coming. The young man said, "I want to accomplish majestic things."

"Very well," the Master said, "Here is a list of the fundamentals of achieving your goal."

- Know the purpose of life is the goal; a life lived on purpose is the journey to the destination." In your journey to becoming a Taoist monk, remember that life is misguided when it focuses on getting and forgets to give; this shifts your thoughts and helps you concentrate on supporting others.

- Know your strengths and what you can do. Realize that some goals require the strengths and abilities you do not have. Think Big. You are stronger than you believe.

- Be willing to do small things in a big way. When you do little things with enthusiasm, you see enormous opportunities. To begin your journey, you must take the first step, another step, and then another step.

- What you do is essential, and so is what you do not do. Move from where you are to where you want to go, focus on projects that bring you closer to your goal, and disregard what is not.

Master Chen said, "There is one last piece of advice I must give you." The young man leaned in, awaiting the Master's last words of wisdom: "If a man dwells on the past, he robs the present. But if a man ignores the past, he may rob the future. The roots of our past nurture the seeds of our destiny."

As the young man and Master Chen parted, he heard the Master say, "As you go forward, you must pass on to others the knowledge you gained to help them find their path to achievement."

Eight Guidelines for Setting Goals

Psychologists use the term "goal gradient" to describe that having a plan pulls you toward the goal, like a magnet.

As you set goals, write out specific goals you want to achieve.

1. **Set specific, measurable goals.** Knowing what you want to do provides a measurement for signaling when you have reached it. Build checkpoints along the way. Decide dates, times, and quantities so you can measure achievement.

2. **Set priorities.** Where you have several goals, give each a priority. Then, review the plans and re-rank until they show the life God wants you to live.

3. **Write goals down so you won't forget them.** Putting a plan into writing makes it more concrete and increases your sense of commitment.

4. **Set realistic goals.** Set goals you can achieve. You won't spend the effort to reach a goal that you perceive to be

unattainable. Set challenging goals that are out of your immediate grasp but not so far that there is no hope of achieving them.

5. **Don't set goals too low.** If you select a goal that is too low, you will feel no challenge in making it, and you will not invest energy and time in pursuing it.

6. **Set goals that relate to your vision.** Ensure the purpose you are working for is something you want, not just something that sounds good.

7. **Set goals aligned with your core values.** You want to be working toward goals that have eternal meaning for you. Setting goals consistent with your values helps lead to success. Establishing goals that differ from your values dilutes the chances of success. Conflict, frustration, and stress can arise when your goals and values need to be aligned.

8. **Commit to achieving the goal.** Stay focused. Once the goal is clear, the other decisions become more natural. Look at all your daily activities through the lens of your goals.

Five Ways to Being Your Best

In the English language, the number 1 is significant. It is the first in a set or series. Businesses strive to be number one in their market; teams and athletes want to be ranked number one in sports.

Being number one may only sometimes be possible. Other people have strengths, talents, positions, education, and opportunities unavailable to you. The wish to be number one is commendable, but not everyone can be number one. A more desirable and achievable goal is to be your best. You become number one by using what you have or gain.

Five steps to being your best:

1. **Be unique.** Know that no one else is like you. You are like your fingerprints, unique. Your education, experiences, and environment make you unique.

2. **Be specific.** Being your best requires focusing on one or two essential things for your purpose and goals. Your actions should bring you closer to achieving the goal. Avoid activities that do not serve the focus.

3. **Be enthusiastic**. Knowing how your contribution contributes to the overall projects helps generate commitment and passion for the job.

4. **Be a team player**. A team's strategy is to unite and contribute the sum of its individual members' best. Each member works for the good of the whole, and the sum is greater than the parts.

5. **Be prepared.** People who do their best continue to receive opportunities to contribute. This commitment leads to more significant assignments, added responsibility, and pay. People who prepare themselves and always bring their best are rare. It is a rarity that determines the value.

Being your best improves those around you. You cannot become a winner without promoting the winning spirit in others.

When You Win, Everyone Wins

Improving yourself improves those around you. You cannot become a winner without promoting the winning spirit in others. There is no solo success. Here are seven steps for improving yourself and those around you.

Choose to Be Positive. Having a positive attitude makes it incredible how circumstances bend to accommodate you. A positive attitude serves as a powerful driver of actions. It causes you to attempt to do more.

Expose Yourself to Something New. People are a product of their education, experiences, entourage, and environment. Successful people use each day to learn something new, try something new, meet someone new, and visit fresh places.

Enjoy Today as If It Were Your Last. See today for what it is: the present and the present guarantee you get. Ask yourself, "Is what I am doing today going to help me achieve my goal?" If the answer is "yes," then keep doing it. If the answer is "no," then redirect your activities.

Define the End of the Day at the beginning of the Day. Spend at least 15 magic minutes first thing each morning, planning your day. The goal is to control your day and not let it control you. Work on what matters, and don't get off track.

Invest in yourself. Investing in yourself keeps you growing and contributing. As you become more valuable, you achieve a reputation as a professional and create a broader influence. Set aside some prime time for investing in yourself regularly.

Execute. Execution is the key to success and bridges the gap between plans and results. Be a doer. Be productive; get the right things done. Don't confuse effectiveness with effort. Focus on results, not activity.

Have Fun and celebrate success. Feel free to celebrate. Significant achievements call for immediate celebration. Celebrating achievement reinforces achievement and leads to further performance. Celebrate progress, not activity.

The Power of Values

When I was six, my vocabulary did not include "values. I did not understand that a unique set of values drove one's behavior. I acted because I acted. But I knew The Lone Ranger fought against evil. I didn't realize that his actions, like Superman's, resulted from their values of Truth, Justice, and the American Way of Life. The Ranger was a hero because he combined the nation's virtues into one man fighting evil.

Today, I long to return to yesteryear, when "Out of the past come the thundering hoof-beats of the great horse Silver." I yearn for the Ranger to ride again. I want to associate with people of integrity, men and women who are truthful, just, joyful, optimistic, enthusiastic, kind, and merciful.

Values have become a rallying cry of the times. We approve of politicians with the "right" values; those we disagree with have "wrong" values. Many Believers equate Christians and good values while tagging non-Christians with less than-good values.

The Dictionary defines values as "Something we esteem or prize;

something of value." Value is a belief, principle, or guide meaningful to a person. It is something you value. "What we obtain too cheap," wrote Thomas Paine, "we esteem too lightly; it is, dearness, only that gives everything its value."

Values set up the ground rules and boundaries of acceptable and desirable behavior. Values show how people act in their daily lives. They help set priorities and decide where we spend our time, with whom, and when to do what. Every person has values.

Personal values include belief in orderliness, commitment, creativity, personal development, independence, honesty, integrity, spirituality, professionalism, teamwork, patriotism, accountability, and courage.

Our values determine our choice of possessions and profession, passions, and how we relate to others. This behavioral coding broadcasts the message: Here's what I value.

Someone said, "Values suggest the ringing words in the Declaration of Independence, 'We hold these truths to be self-evident.'"

Successful People Color Outside the Lines

Although you didn't ask for my advice, people seldom do. Here's something to keep you awake at night. According to a recent ranking at Amazon, five out of the top 10 best-selling books in the U.S. last year were adult coloring books. The problem with an adult coloring book or any coloring book is that you must stay within the lines when you color. It's not clear why people color within the lines. Innovative businesses — I suppose all organizations — are looking for out-of-the-box thinkers.

A business needs more job skills to be provided. People looking for employment or a better-paying job aren't engaged in self-learning. According to The Robert Brewer organization, 42% of college graduates never read another book after college. Also, 80% of U.S. families did not buy or read a book last year.

The World Economic Forum's Future of Jobs Report, "The Top 10 skills needed in 2020 compared to the skills required in 2015." The top three skills currently needed are (1) Complex Problem Solving, (2) Coordinating with Others, and (3) People Management. The skills required in 2020 are (1) Complex Problem Solving, (2) Critical Thinking, and (3) Creativity.

If our educational system isn't teaching the skills currently needed, students' burden of learning falls. If you are employed or looking for employment, take Jiddu Krishnamurti's words to heart: "Keep learning and never stop. Not that you read a book, pass an examination, and finish with education. The whole life is a learning process from the moment you are born to the moment you die."

I have several bookcases filled with books but no coloring books. I've read 98% of those books, scanned the other 2%, and determined I wasn't interested. I've learned more from reading books than I gained in school—from the first grade to completing Graduate School.

A good job and a sense of achievement are in your hands. Learning and preparing for a new year is not only about reading books. It's about utilizing all forms of visual and audio media.

I Will Get That Bone Too

I'm thinking about the stories I read as a child. The stories that stand out to me are short and teach a lesson about success and happiness.

Aesop's fable "The Dog and His Bone" contains a lesson for personal success: when we are not content with what we have and grasp for more, we often lose what we have. The fable is about a dog that finds a bone. The dog is so possessive of the bone that he growls at anyone attempting to take it out of his mouth. The dog's attitude is, "This one is mine!"

When the dog went to bury his prized possession, he happened upon a stream. As he looked into the water, he saw his reflection. Thinking it was another dog with a more significant bone, he growled at the reflection, and the dog's reflection growled back. I want that bone, thought the greedy dog, opening his mouth to grasp it. When he did, he lost the bone in his mouth to search for the more extensive bone that did not exist.

People are like that. They have shelter, food, and clothing; they meet their basic needs. But they want the more essential items when they see someone with a bigger house, eating at the finest restaurants, and wearing designer clothes.

The story of the dog emphasizes the foolishness of trading what you have for false promises. Some people enjoy where they live, the food they eat, and their clothes. Other people want to improve in all areas of their lives.

Here are three principles for getting a more prominent bone.

- Protect the bone you have. The bone you have is better than the bone illusion in the water. Focus on what you have.

- Stop wanting and start doing. Once you know your goal, act on it. The bottom line is, are you willing to go after the more significant bone? Too many people only want to want.

- Avoid envy. A bone in your mouth is better than a more prominent "bone" in the water.

Do You Get It Done?

My son, a Lt. Colonel in the United States Army, was so impressed with the book, "A Message to Garcia," that he gave a copy to all his lieutenants as a Captain. When presenting them with the book, he would tell them, "There are some people who deliver the goods. They are the people who get it done! That's what the Army and I expect of you."

The inspiring story of A Message to Garcia is about Colonel Andrew Summers Rowan. He was a young lieutenant in the United States Army when the Spanish-American War broke out. They chose Rowan to deliver a message from President McKinley to General Calixto Garcia, the leader of the revolutionary forces. Author Elbert Hubbard set the stage for the drama and wrote in his 1899 essay, "Garcia was somewhere in the mountain vastness of Cuba — no one knows where. No mail or telegraph message could reach him. The President must secure his cooperation and quickly."

Lieutenant Rowan held the lowest commission rank in the Army. By having his name suggested to the President, Lieutenant Rowan received the ultimate commendation, "If anybody can find Garcia, it is Rowan."

After receiving his instructions to deliver the message to Garcia, Lieutenant Rowan shook his commander's hand. And without asking one question, he sailed to Cuba with no help or directions other than to deliver the President's message. Rowan made his way into the interior mountains with the help of Cuban patriots. He had the President's message to Garcia. The lieutenant faced many obstacles. Elbert Hubbard writes, "The lieutenant's courage and spirit enabled him to succeed."

Elbert Hubbard penned A Message to Garcia over 100 years ago. Over 40 million copies have been sold, and the book has been translated into 37 languages, making it one of the highest-selling books in history. Maybe the message of this "old" essay is a new message that I deliver. It will help if you read the book. Download it, ship it overnight, or purchase it at a bookstore. If you want to own this book, don't check it out of the library. I support libraries, but they frown on underlining and highlighting in their books.

If you are a Lieutenant Rowan, do not hide. Businesses and organizations need people with courage and firm determination.

For Success, Nothing Beats Preparation

When a company offers you employment, what are they proposing? They do not imply job security, advancement, training, or scheduled raises. The offer is: a specific job requires skills and knowledge. We hope you meet the requirements. If you are successful, we will pay you for your contribution. You can continue contributing if you contribute and get a decent return on our investment.

The company expects ongoing positive results, and you provide the results or find you're unemployed. Harsh? Not really. It is primary supply and demand. The company supplies you with a job; in return, they demand results. Though not a great motivation tool, it partially motivates the first two levels of Maslow's Hierarchy of Needs: Psychological and Safety. This type of employee supply/demand motivation works to a degree in the short term.

The worst thing about employee supply/demand is that many employees do not realize that the system works for them by focusing on the "demand" part, improving their skills, and maximizing their strengths. Many people are seeking employment. So, supply is high. Demand will determine who gets the position. The more you are in demand (offering added value), the better the odds of getting hired.

This employee value-added concept applies to people seeking employment and current employees wanting to advance with their company. Most often, the job advancement opportunity goes to the person best prepared. George S. Clauson, the author of "The Richest Man in Babylon," made this point: "Opportunity is a haughty goddess who wastes no time with those who are unprepared."

Every day, people, especially those who won't take responsibility for their position on the food chain, cannot take advantage of improving themselves. Self-development is just that: Self-development. Successful people accept that continued success—personal and professional- depends on continuous learning. And they have a daily plan for self-improvement. What book or magazine have you read today? What video are you viewing, or what CD do you listen to that improves your mind and increases your demand qualifications?

Set Goals for Success

I don't think I have met anyone whose goal is to fail. But failure happens. Our response to loss determines whether we become successful. Writing "success" and "failure" in the same sentence is strange. Winston Churchill did when he noted, "Success is going from failure to failure without loss of enthusiasm."

When people fail, they learn from experience and then move on—the wiser—to try again. They don't see failure as a final but as a learning experience.

I suggest eleven ideas for success.

- Determine where you want to be at the end of the current year. If you know your goal, you can work backward, setting small, specific, well-planned actions to achieve it and moving toward it with each action step.

- Establish accountability. Accept responsibility and accountability for your actions. While others may help you, the buck stops with you.

- Expect and prepare for the unexpected. Peter's Law states, "The unexpected always happens." Before finalizing your goals, conduct a "What if" exercise. If this happens, I will do this. Anticipate and be ready for when "stuff" happens.

- Manage your time. Make all 1,440 minutes count every day. Successful people stay focused on their goals but do not spend all their time working. Strive for balance.

- Develop a can-do attitude. A positive attitude generates genuine enthusiasm. A positive attitude is essential for success.

- Have an innovative spirit. Always look for ways to innovate and improve every activity you engage in.

- Keep your knowledge current and your skills marketable. Engage in continuous self-improvement. Reading for personal growth is part of a successful person's life.

- Be a problem solver. Discover new and innovative ways to remove obstacles and accomplish your tasks. Do not be a problem conveyor; be recognized as a solutions ambassador.

- Focus on results, not on being busy. Develop the ability to get things done to achieve your goals. Never confuse activity with results. Engage in activities that advance you to your goal and avoid activities that detract from it.

- Celebrate and have fun. Your goal should be to celebrate the results, not the activities.

Self-Discipline Precedes Self-Improvement

"In reading the lives of prominent men, I found that the first victory they won was over themselves... self-discipline with all of them came first." — Harry S. Truman.

Before writing this story, I could not tell you that there are over 1,100,000 English words, with a new word created every 98 minutes or about 14.7 words daily. This information helps me know that 3.6 new English words will be born when I finish this article.

When I asked her its meaning, I often thought of my maternal grandmother's instructions; her reply was always, "Look it up in the Dictionary." This article is about self-discipline being the foundation for self-improvement. So, I began by looking up "self-discipline." Merriam-Webster's Collegiate Dictionary defines "self-discipline" as "Correction or regulation of oneself for improvement." Roget offers "constraint, "control," and "discretion" as synonyms. The ancient Greek philosopher Plato said, "The first and best victory is to conquer self."

If I had to pick a topic that interests me most, self-improvement might be it. Information regarding self-discipline might be the least interesting. Even St. Paul lists self-control as the last of the nine fruits of the Spirit.

Several dictionaries and a Thesaurus are on my bookshelf. There is always a definition to look up or a synonym needed. Words make up a lot of my day. I choose the right word when I am writing or speaking. Sometimes, I fail, but I cannot blame it on a dictionary or thesaurus. Self-discipline is the culprit. To use the "right" word takes self-discipline to search one of those dictionaries or Thesaurus.

People want success but are unwilling to discipline themselves; they still need to be successful. The challenge for talent and exceptional strength is to control and manage these assets.

Self-discipline allows us to experience self-improvement, discover ourselves, and gain knowledge. Theodore Roosevelt captures the essence of this article. His quote inspires you: "With self-discipline, most anything is possible."

That Reminds Me of A Story

Seven Reasons Why People Fail to Plan

"Failing to plan is planning to fail." — Alan Lakein

Many people are familiar with the process of business or military planning. A growing number have experience setting goals, developing strategies, and listing the action steps needed to achieve the goal. However, few people have applied the planning process to their personal lives. Personal planning can shape the way you approach your daily life.

Despite the benefits of personal planning, only a few people do it. There are many reasons people need help with planning. Here are seven:

1. Planning is not a priority. This excuse often comes disguised as "I don't have enough time to plan." Everyone has the same time, 24 hours each day. The question is not more or less time; it is how you spend your time.

2. Lack of planning expertise. Planning involves simple steps: 1. Know where you are, 2. Know where you want to go, 3. Devise a method for getting to your target. Some people need to know if they should make personal plans or even how to develop strategies. These people can access how-to information—books, magazines, the internet, and friends—on planning.

3. Apathy or indifference. This reaction is the response of the

fatalist. In their opinion, whatever is to will be. So, don't make plans for tomorrow. If it does not convince you that planning will make a difference and help you achieve your goal, you will not put effort into developing it. A hazard to personal planning is an inert person.

4. Believing that planning is a straitjacket. People cannot plan because they want to avoid feeling boxed in. In the past, not meeting goals made them feel like failures. Therefore, they refrain from being measured against a benchmark to prevent further failures.

5. Resistance to change. People often resist change because they are still determining their ability to take on new roles. Sometimes, people prefer the status quo to something new, even when the situation is inadequate. We seldom motivate people who do not want change to seek change.

6. Fear of failure. A lack of self-confidence is always a contributor to a failure to plan. Even if it doesn't work, attempting something new opens doors that would have otherwise remained closed. Overcome fear by doing what you fear.

7. People need to prepare to work to achieve their goals. The first 80% of goal achievement is the determination to do it and not compromise; you stay focused on the plan no matter the roadblocks. The difference between success and failure planning

is, "How much passion, commitment, and enthusiasm did the planner have?"

There is nothing mysterious, complicated, or revolutionary about personal planning. The process works if you dedicate yourself to it. The individual plan can shape the way you approach your daily life.

In developing a personal success plan, look for a good one, and do not waste time creating a perfect one. General George S. Patton said, "A good plan today is better than a perfect plan tomorrow."

Be A Difference Maker

In the classic song "What A Difference A Day Makes," Dinah Washington sings, "What a difference a day makes, twenty-four little hours Brought the sun and flowers where there used to be rain." These words remind me that creative actions can quickly produce significant differences.

Some people opt out when confronted with an opportunity to make a difference. They choose the ordinary. Mediocrity is an anathema to a Difference Maker if you want to create a difference.

Difference Makers believe that their actions, not those of someone else, cause success or failure. Therefore, to be a Difference Maker, you must:

- Be willing to take risks. Do not allow fear to overcome your desire to make a difference.

- Keep up with the latest technologies and innovations in your field. At a minimum, you must continuously develop your skills that lead to the next level.

- Be passionate about what you do. A competitive spirit under control can move mountains.

- Commit to what you are doing.

- Provide answers to the problems. Many people are problem-bearers. A Difference Maker identifies the real problem and suggests plausible solutions.

- Seek counsel from other stakeholders and be open to adjusting or corrections to your proposed plan.

- Be service-oriented. Make the lives of customers and associates better, more comfortable, and more rewarding.

If you aren't making a difference in your position, maybe you aren't in the right place or the person for the job. Either you or your employer must correct this untenable situation. "Don't let what you cannot do," wrote John Wooden, "interfere with what you can do." Anyone with talent and desire can make a difference, given that they can do so. If unable to create a difference, consider changing jobs or organizations.

Making a difference is something you can do every day. There's much truth in the old Spanish proverb: "It's not the same to talk of bulls as to be in the bullring." To make a difference, you must take part.

You will only know the difference you can make once you make a difference. In creating a difference, you become a better person and come closer to achieving your purpose for being on planet Earth.

Choose to be known as a Difference Maker. Challenge yourself to go out each day and make a difference by answering these three questions:

1. What will I do today to make a difference?
2. What am I doing today to make a difference?
3. What did I do today to make a difference?

Read Up. Speak Up and Rise Above the Ordinary

Many people no longer read, and others have lost the desire to read.

Reading is excellent for you. Applying what you read is better. As Socrates pointed out, "Employ your time in improving yourself by other men's writings so that you shall come easily by what others have labored hard for." Or, as Roald Dahl proclaimed, "If you are going to get anywhere in life, read many books."

Many people speak up using information drawn from a shallow well. Others speak up and rise above the ordinary operating data pulled from a deep and boundless well.

Whether you are a man or a woman who cannot find your voice or just someone looking for that extra inspiration, let John Lewis's words bring out your voice every day. "When you see something that is not right, not fair, not just, speak up. Say something; you must do something."

Don't let your lack of knowledge and fear of speaking up ruin your life. Read a book this month.

Think Positive

When you least expect it, a negative thought can pop into your mind and cause you to fail.

Many years ago, I read a story called "The Wallenda Factor." It was a tragic story about Karl Wallenda and his famous high-wire walk in San Juan, Puerto Rico. It was his last performance. At 85, Wallenda lost his balance and fell to his death.

After his death, his widow said, "All Karl thought about for three straight months before the accident was falling. Instead of walking the tightrope, he seemed to put all his energy into not falling."

Positive thinking is a mindset that anyone can learn and develop. Start by replacing negative thoughts with positive ones. Instead of thinking I am a failure, replace negative thinking with positive thoughts. I failed, but I will learn from my mistakes. Willie Nelson famously said, "Once you replace negative thoughts with positive ones, you'll start having positive results."

Believe in Yourself

Some years ago, my wife and I went to dinner. We were newlyweds, and dinner out meant hamburgers, pizza, or KFC chicken. As we walked down the streets in downtown Atlanta, we saw a man in a white suit carrying a cane. It was Colonel Harland Sanders of Kentucky Fried Chicken fame.

We approached Colonel Sanders and introduced ourselves. Life only gives you a few opportunities to meet celebrities when you are 26 and making $95 a week. He asked us whether we knew of a beautiful seafood restaurant nearby. We didn't. Here is the owner of KFC looking for a seafood restaurant.

The Colonel is an excellent example of someone who believes in their ability to succeed, is persistent, and stays focused.

Colonel Sanders perfected his "Secret Recipe" after many trials. The Colonel had faith in himself and, through his humble start at a Shell Service Station in 1930, succeeded with over 25,000 KFC restaurants in over 145 countries.

Step out of your comfort zone. Only those who dare to succeed can succeed. You never know what opportunities a new day offers. Success could be today.

Who is On Your Happiness Bus?

The passengers on your happiness bus contribute to who you are and what you become. As the bus driver and owner, you determine who rides on it.

Some people are already on your bus, and some are waiting to board. Sell tickets to positive people and remove negative passengers.

Toxic Passengers.

Toxic passengers will slowly drain the life out of you and pollute everyone on the bus. Eliminating these hostile passengers will allow for more energy on your bus.

Complaining Passengers.

You probably have a complainer passenger who never sees the rainbow, only the rain.

That Reminds Me of A Story

Passengers who want to bring you down.

Some passengers attempt to make you feel uncomfortable whenever they are on the bus. It is as if they were born to humiliate you and impede your success and happiness. This passenger always drags you down and meddles with your dreams and goals.

Symbiotic relationship passengers.

These passengers strive for a mutual relationship. They gain from knowing you, while you earn from mentoring them.

Encouragers

Some passengers give support, foster confidence, and bring hope. These bus riders consistently seek to understand you and your hopes and dreams. Great encouragers help bring out the best in you.

Having the right passengers on your bus can lead to a happy journey. Remove the unruly and misfit passengers from your bus. It's rare for passengers to change their behavior. It is your bus, and you determine the passengers. Choose wisely.

Tips on Public Speaking

"If I returned to college again, I'd concentrate on two areas: learning to write and speak before an audience. Nothing in life is more important than communicating effectively." -Gerald R. Ford.

A memory came back to me this morning. It is a crucial memory. It was about a defining moment when I realized public speaking wasn't to fear but to enjoy. Early in my career, I attended a business meeting with a group of project managers to discuss their projects. Suddenly, one manager, overcome with passion, gave an emotional speech about his project. His words ignited the meeting, transforming it from dull facts to inspiring goals, purpose, strategies, and actions. After his presentation, the other project managers stood and applauded him.

I liked that.

Strangely, most adults have a fear of public speaking. Some people would rather die than stand before an audience and speak. Even though they may have something to say, they are concerned with how others perceive and evaluate them.

Don't allow your thoughts about how others perceive you to dilute your confidence when you make a public speech. Be more concerned with how you perceive yourself.

Of all the poor deals humans receive, one must evaluate themselves by what others think, not their beliefs. People have a lot of stories and wisdom to share. When asked for his secret to public speaking, a public speaker said, "Have something to say, say it, and sit down."

Nothing is more exhilarating than standing before an audience and hearing their applause. To close this story, I use Franklin D. Roosevelt's advice on public speaking: "Be sincere; be brief; be seated."

Seldom Are We Honest with Ourselves

Seldom are we honest with ourselves about our self-improvement plans. For example, when an overweight person commits to losing 10 pounds per month for the first six months of the new year, they haven't counted the price they will pay to lose those 60 pounds. A pound of fat equals 3,500 calories, so to lose 60 pounds, you must burn 210,000 more calories than you consume. Wishing for and hoping for are not methods for dropping 60 pounds in six months.

Another resolution that proves hard to keep is to improve our self-image. How we see ourselves has a powerful impact on happiness. People have looked at themselves for so long that they only glance at themselves as they are today, not what they can become.

Lifestyle or behavior is an entrenched habit many people want to improve by improving their self-image. I have a list of 20 affirmations I read daily, sometimes twice daily, that may help you enhance your self-image and fulfill your resolutions.

Positive Affirmations.

I Can reflect on my purpose in everything I do.

I Can learn to be fair to myself.

I Can encourage myself.

I Can believe in myself.

I Can accept change.

I Can get outside of my comfort zone.

I Can do things as they come up.

I Can focus on the positive.

I Can forgive myself and others.

I Can accept myself for who I am.

I Can go for good enough.

I Can stay the course.

I Can learn new things.

I Can live in the moment. Nothing happens next.

I Can practice self-forgiveness.

I Can move on from the past.

That Reminds Me of A Story

I Can stop worrying.

I Can cut myself some slack.

You lose weight when you consume fewer calories than you burn. You get control of your life when you think more positively and less negatively.

A Professional

As she explained the pros and cons of our new home and the benefits of living in Walterboro, SC, our realtor impressed me with her sales ability. I asked if she had read "Death of a Salesman?" She said, "Yes."

Death of a Salesman follows the life of Willy Loman, a struggling salesperson, and explores some key points and how they can apply to everyday life. The story is a heartbreaking exploration of human struggles, aspirations, and the complexities of family life. By reflecting on the key points of "Death of a Salesman," you can gain insights into your life and make more informed decisions.

Willy Loman strives for the American Dream, which means anyone can succeed through hard work. The book shows how unrealistic expectations and mindless ambition can lead to dissatisfaction. In everyday life, it's essential to have goals and dreams, but it's equally important to be realistic and adapt when necessary.

Willy's money problems and ambition hurt his mental health and relationships with his family. This serves as a reminder that financial stress can profoundly affect individuals and their loved ones. Economic stability and responsible money management are essential to avoid problems.

- The Destructive Nature of Pride and Ego: Willy's excessive pride and inability to accept help or criticism contribute to his downfall. His belief in being well-liked and admired overshadows his actual sales skills. Personal growth and success can come from being open to feedback, acknowledging weaknesses, and seeking help.

- The Illusion of Success: Willy's obsession with appearance and success leads him to live in a world of illusions and self-deception. He constantly embellishes stories to maintain the image of a successful salesperson, even when the reality is quite different. Being genuine and authentic in everyday life, embracing successes and failures, is crucial.

- Legacy and Impact: The book raises questions about the legacy one leaves behind and the impact of one's actions on future generations. In everyday life, we must consider the consequences of our actions and strive to leave a positive legacy.

SECTION 4: THE POWER OF MOTIVATION

Everyone needs stories that motivate.

The Caravan Story

One night, a small caravan of people was crossing a desert. The night was unusually dark; it was a quarter moon. Suddenly, a voice spoke out of the heavens about midnight, commanding the travelers to stop and dismount.

Once on the ground, the voice instructed them to pick up rocks and place them in their saddlebags. If they followed this instruction, they would be both glad and sad when the sun came up in the morning. Doing as told, they remounted their camels.

The travelers dismounted and carefully opened their saddlebags at the first sign of light. They gladly discovered that the rocks they had picked up had turned into gold inside the bags during the night. But the gladness was short-lived because they realized they should have collected more rocks.

I'm confident that nearly everyone wishes they had collected more rocks. We are aware of individuals who initially failed to gather enough rocks but later, when given another opportunity, gathered additional rocks that turned out to be valuable gold.

To ensure progress, it's advisable to start each morning by asking yourself what your goal for the day is: collecting rocks. At the end of each day, take a moment to review those goals and ask yourself if you have gathered enough rocks to accomplish your goal.

That Reminds Me of A Story

The Rope Story

Every circus has elephants. No matter that, they also had clowns, tigers, and dancing dogs. But elephants, the largest land mammals, draw the attention of boys and girls. Each elephant has a story to tell. The best story I remember is the elephant rope story.

For years, I believed in the elephant rope story and how motivational speakers used it to illustrate unlimited boundaries. We can break the "rope" tied to our past.

The story illustrates that when a rope ties a baby elephant to a small stake driven into the ground, the elephant roams out to the rope's length. The young elephant has not developed its strength and cannot pull up the stake.

As the elephant grows, he doesn't have an ah-ha moment and realizes he could easily break free from his bond. So, they condition him to stay within his known boundary, and he doesn't venture out.

Wild elephants live in families called herds and find it difficult to leave the other group members, and they often suffer from their boundary conditioning; they stay with the familiar. However, these large land mammals have three distinct personality traits: attentiveness, sociability, and aggressiveness.

If you are into elephant learning, consider applying the lessons of the elephant's personality.

Attentiveness. Be thoughtful of everyone with whom you come into contact. Don't prejudge others. Please get to know them and then evaluate them.

Social. Be friendly and warm; you attract more people to your cause.

Aggressiveness. Be forceful and assertive, but also listen to others' opinions. The tactic of hearing more and talking less is excellent advice.

Step outside your rope zone and test the boundaries. Don't follow the other elephants. While others mean well, it is possible that you need a fresh path. When someone compliments you by saying, "You have a memory like an elephant," they tell you have an excellent memory. Unlike the elephant, don't let imaginary ropes and small stakes define you.

Don't Fear Tomorrow. Be Fearful You Will Miss Today

One of the greatest crimes many people commit is their failure to live today because they fear tomorrow.

In school, they teach us that people are born with a minimal number of instinctive fears—of falling, loud noise, and darkness. These are there to help us survive. They do not teach us that another fear has the power to stagnate our lives, careers, relationships, and success.

That Reminds Me of A Story

That fear is the fear of the future.

We fear tomorrow because tomorrow is unknown. We do not understand what may happen, and people think the worst. The fear of tomorrow exists in our minds. There is little or no evidence of what tomorrow may bring. We have no guarantee of tomorrow. The way to overcome fears tomorrow is to become so involved in today that you forget to be afraid.

The only reality is the present, which will soon be the past, just as what you thought was the future becomes the present. It doesn't matter whether you are rich, poor, or in between; you can only live in the moment. It's these moments that record successes or past failures. You think of the future, and that moment becomes a reality.

You can't change the past or relive it; however, some people try to rewrite it. You can't predict the future, but you can always find someone willing to play a prophet's role for a fee or promise of notoriety.

Thomas Edison didn't worry about yesterday's failures, nor did he leave his success in the future. Edison applied himself to the task at hand. After 10,000 failed tries to develop the electric light bulb, his victory came when the light bulb glowed. Today, the world would be more miserable and different if Edison had lived based on regret and not hope. People have a brighter today because Edison lived in the present.

Rodin's sculpture, The Thinker, is an excellent picture of someone who worries about the future and is stuck in the present. While we contemplate the future, the present is changing. What was tomorrow is now today? Life's reality confirms the Greek philosopher Heraclitus's statement: "The only constant is change." So, if you want to be a success, don't worry about tomorrow; handle today, and before you know it, tomorrow's dread becomes today's opportunity.

First Row a Little Boat

Sometimes, I buy a book because the title attracts me. One such book, "First You Have to Row a Little Boat," caught my attention. The title revealed the book: crawling before walking, walking before running. Placing fundamentals first is another way of saying the first things first.

People repeatedly believe they can skip the fundamentals and become a success overnight. I have never sailed a boat—little or big—but I have experienced attempting to overlook the small steps and aim for the final goal.

Look at every day, week, month, and year as an opportunity to improve yourself.

When we underestimate the steps involved in growing, the example of planting seeds comes to mind. There are five essential and sequential steps required to produce a flower. The five keys are necessary for developing personal success.

1. Plant the seed in fertile ground. Don't be surprised when weeds of defeat and discouragement spring up among your planted seeds. Goal-minded people know to expect and plan for adversity.

2. Fertilize and water. The flower doesn't appear overnight. Don't become discouraged and quit. Success takes time, hard work, and concentration, like learning to row a small boat.

3. Embrace change. Give the seed time to grow. Have faith, and don't accept the criticism of others. Like the little plant, you will burst into a new environment one day.

4. Concentrate on the first three steps, and you will reap the fruits of success. Celebrate your success.

5. Replant. Look for future growth. There are more incredible things ahead. The seed of one successful replant carries the seeds of the next.

Success begins with successfully rowing a little boat or planting seeds. Sow the seeds of hard work and learn the fundamentals—determine your goal and focus on achieving it—and you will excel.

Wayne Nalls

The Lazy Man's Way to Riches

The ad in the magazine I read broke the copywriting rules I learned at the University of Florida.

People rarely read all-copy ads, especially a full page of text. The ad should have a mix of text, photos, and illustrations. The combination of type and image should follow the AIDA rule: attention, interest, desire, and action. The copy should be short, sentences; your goal was not to lose the reader's attention. I read a page advertisement containing only text and some long sentences. The ad headline read, "The Lazy Man's Way to Riches," was copy-perfect and captured my attention. Here was the secret to getting rich and doing nothing.

I mailed my ten dollars to the address in the ad and waited for the book. The book's advice was to write a book as the author did, advertise it, and watch the money accumulate. Joe paid fifty cents for printing his book, creating revenues of over $1,000,000.

The Bible presents another and opposite view of laziness. The writer of Proverbs says, "Go to the ant, you slacker! Observe its ways and become wise. Without a leader, administrator, or ruler, it prepares its provisions in summer and gathers food during harvest. How long will you stay in bed, you slacker? When will you get up from your sleep? A little sleep, a little slumber, a little folding of the arms to rest, and your poverty will come like a robber, your need, like a bandit." (Proverbs 6:6-11, HCSB)

I'm not lazy, and something is satisfying about getting a job done. Sitting on my front porch and watching the flag flowing in the breeze while I do nothing else is satisfying. And then God reminds me of the ways of the ant.

How to Make Better Decisions

My son, who lives in Alexandria, VA, shared this story. He was out Jogging early in the morning when he encountered a young couple of bicycle riders. They had stopped and appeared confused. So, he asked them if he could help them. "Yes," the young male replied. "We don't know where to start." My son asked them, "Where do you want to go?" The female said, "We want to bicycle to the Capital." "Well, you're on the right path," my son replied. "Follow it until you come to the fork in the trail. Then, take either path. Both lead to the Capital. Though you may take the right fork, it's more scenic."

When businesspeople come to a fork in the road and decide, they search for more than a scenic path.

Seven ideas to help you make better decisions:

1. Get advice from decision-makers you trust. Don't be

stubborn. There are people more intelligent than you and with more decision-making experience.

2. Be sure of the facts; weigh all the variables. Identify the relevant information and discard the rest.

3. Faced with a decision, choose wisely. You are free to determine, but you are responsible for the results of your choice. A person needs help to decide to keep up with the advances in their career, but they need to catch up in their job.

4. Learn from your past decisions. Follow up on the outcome. When you follow up, you gain new experience that helps with the next choice.

5. If possible, don't rush decisions. Often, problems will solve themselves. If the situation is essential and urgent, don't procrastinate. The right decision executed today is better than a superior choice next week.

6. Trust your instinct.

7. Accept responsibility, regardless of the outcome.

As for jogging, bicycling, or giving directions, I leave that to someone else.

That Reminds Me of A Story

Facing Up to Obstacles

We should take the advice of the author Frank Clark, "If you find a path with no obstacles, it probably doesn't lead anywhere."

A friend of mine told me an excellent story about overcoming obstacles. When he was in high school, he had a problem understanding chemistry.

He studied twice as hard as he did for other classes and asked a classmate to tutor him. He also met with friends the night before any exam to discuss the material that could be on the test. Nothing helped to improve his grades.

The grumpy, older chemistry teacher repeatedly declared that student problems did not trouble him. His philosophy was, "I teach it, you learn it."

The teacher who had struck fear into my friend was the obstacle between my friend and a passing grade. He had two choices: ignore the barrier and fail the course or make an appointment to see the teacher and hope for help. He requested a meeting. To his surprise, the teacher greeted him, smiled, and asked how he could help. After the greeting's shock, my friend told the teacher, "I just don't get chemistry."

"Good," the teacher said. We are halfway home; you know and own the problem. You recognize it as an internal obstacle you have direct control over. Let's discover why you are not fond of chemistry. After asking several why questions, I found the real reason: I was not too fond of chemistry. My parents wanted me to be a doctor, and medical schools require a knowledge of chemistry. I want to be an entrepreneur and grow businesses where knowledge of chemistry isn't' required.

The obstacle to doing well in chemistry was that my friend wanted to be something other than what his parents wanted him to be: a doctor. His heart was into entrepreneurship, not medicine.

Obstacles make people uncomfortable. But we often find growth opportunities in the challenges we face. How do you see obstacles?

Before You Say It Cannot Be Done

Fortunately, I keep newspaper and magazine clippings of examples of people with a positive can-do attitude. Here is an example of an article from January 2018. Secretary of Defense General James Mattis exhibited what it means to get things done.

He scheduled himself to speak at the Johns Hopkins School of Advanced International Studies. However, the secretary incurred travel obstacles to his speaking engagement, making him late. Rather than calling and saying, "I'll be late because of circumstances," Mattis and his staff exited their vehicle. They walked on the sidewalk for 15 minutes of his trip to the Johns Hopkins School of Advanced International Studies.

It was a sight. Six men strolled down the sidewalk: Mattis, three military assistants dressed in uniform, and two civilian staff members.

You'll pardon me for saying so, but our President and Congress can learn a lot by walking some sidewalks in Washington. They may even gain a MUST DO attitude.

Examples are great; we can all learn from the Secretary's example. Incorporate the MUST-DO attitude. It should not matter whether you are a Republican or Democrat, female or male, poor or rich, uneducated or educated.

You must have a must-do attitude and not worry about recognition. Just do it!

I Haven't Had a Chance

Few live by the rule, "Don't judge a book by its cover. Most people understand this metaphor:" You shouldn't presume the worth or value of something by its outward appearance alone." We're used to prejudging people, actions, books, and intentions, and often, we do not make new friends, make correct decisions, and read inspiring books.

In his best-selling book Blink, Malcolm Gladwell wrote about intuitive thought and the first two seconds of judgment. This internal computer—our brain — "quickly and quietly processes as much data we need to function as human beings." Gladwell used the example of a person in the middle of a street who sees a truck bearing down on him and doesn't have time to think through his options. He reacts. I would leap out of the truck's way without thinking about it.

Do You Like Britain's Got Talent

The show predetermines the singers' fates based on age, song style, and interview performance. The singer often shocks the judges, including Simon Cowell, when they hear them singing "I Dreamed a Dream," "No Regrets," and "Think."

When asked why they haven't recorded or discovered before, many say, "I haven't had a chance." "No one allowed me to sing before." These constants prove you're never too old to follow your dream.

These contestants have a hidden talent, and so do you. Just as there are no duplicate fingerprints, there is no one else with your skills, dreams, willingness to work, and unquenchable thirst; you must be your best — no matter the opinions of others.

That Reminds Me of A Story

Eliminate the Participation Trophy

I remember a brilliant movie titled "The Usual Suspects." The 1995 film contained some memorable lines. My favorite quote is, "The greatest trick the devil ever pulled was convincing the world he did not exist." I haven't thought about that quote for a long time. These are the words of a top-notch professional salesperson.

Not to be outdone by the devil, today's world uses that same line, slightly changed. The greatest trick the world ever pulled was convincing people that there were no losers; everyone gets a trophy. That everyone receives an award for participating seems wrong to me.

The participants, even the sluggards — know before the event that a trophy awaits them. This reward method is not challenging; it is a cop-out.

By doing this, we:

1. Destroy the trophy's value.
2. Mislead the participants into believing that all they must do to get an award is to show up.
3. The players who do not win will never know the taste of victory (nor the smell of defeat).

Forget the Wake, Steer the Boat, and Keep Your Eyes on the Goal

When people experience a lack of motivation, it is easy to lie down and wallow in the mud as often as we do. They look around and see gloom, doom, and despair everywhere. Once they envisioned a bright future, they now look backward at all the pressing problems and draw them away from their goals.

But the answer to achieving goals lies in something other than the past. It would help if you did not believe the past drives your future. Past failures are just that—past failures. What you did yesterday, last week or last month does not have to influence you today.

For example, the wake of a boat does nothing to propel it forward. A boater who continually watches the wake heads for trouble. Successful boaters forget the wake, steer the boat, trim the sails, and keep their eyes on the goal. Professionals must forget the past, execute action plans, monitor and adjust activities according to the territory's winds, and stay focused on the destination.

Focusing on the goal can trim or eliminate actions that sidetrack you from achieving it. Therefore, you can align your actions with your goals. Reaching your goals—business and personal—defines the life you live. Failing to achieve your goals also explains the life you live.

That Reminds Me of A Story

The "keep your eyes on the goal" admonition assumes you have a goal or destination. As an American film producer and director Cecil B. DeMille remarked, "The person who makes a success out of living is the one who sees his goal steadily and aims for it unswervingly." Business executive and author Harvey Mackay said, "If you don't have a destination, you'll never get there." Before we can reach a goal, we must have a goal.

Often, we confuse "wants" and "wishes" with goals. These reveries frequently originate in the past with the wake. Benjamin Mays observed, "The tragedy of life does not lie in not reaching your goal. The tragedy lies in having no goal to reach."

Your most important goal should be to live a life worth living. Author John Alston explained, "The dash between the birth year and year of death on a tombstone represents a person's entire life—and it's important to make sure it means something." What will your dash represent?

Job Passion

Merriam-Webster's Collegiate Dictionary defines passion as a powerful feeling or belief. Synonyms are enthusiasm, zeal, fervor, intensity, and gusto." Passion is the ingredient most missing in today's workers. The lack of job desire always leads to two questions:

1. Why do I do this job?

2. Is this all there is?

Unhappy employees need to extend themselves. They master the art of looking busy but contributing little. They are going through the motions and deceiving themselves and their employer. When you are unhappy at work, it has a massive effect on the rest of your life.

Passion creates excitement about arriving in the morning, being productive, and contributing to the team effort. Passion makes people cheerful.

People need a reason for acting. The more critical the purpose, the more likely we will accomplish the task. You can create passion and achieve almost any goal with a significant purpose.

Use "And" More Often Than "But"

A retired baseball coach said, "When I noticed my pitcher was having trouble, I called time out and went to the mound to help him calm down. We discussed how the game was going well and complimented his ability to operate under pressure. My last advice to him was: "But, whatever you do, don't throw the batter a high fastball."

That Reminds Me of A Story

I no sooner returned to the dugout and sat down when I saw my pitcher throw a high fastball and heard the bat meeting the ball. Home run! I gave my pitcher clear directions not to pitch a high fastball. He registered the last words in the pitcher's mind: a high fastball. He did not remember the "but don't."

People remember our last words, mostly when we are speaking words of praise. The term "and" connects the praise with the expectation of more. So, why dilute a compliment or praise by inserting the word "but"?

When you use the word, *but* after a compliment, you say to the other person, "You did less than expected." The report was good, but it could have been better. "But" connects praise with criticism. Using *and* acknowledges and communicates, I know you can improve.

In the first book of the Bible, God uses "and" thirteen times in the first twelve verses of Genesis, chapter 1. He says, "There is more to come."

Negative: Managers compliment employees on a report and then say, "But you need to improve your spelling."

Positive: Managers compliment employees on a report and then say you will improve your spelling with each report.

Negative: Parents say to their children, "That is an excellent report," "But." They communicate that their grades, while good, are not good enough.

Positive: Parents said to their children, "That's a good report," and communicated that good grades are a sign that the best is yet to come.

Acknowledging and releasing yourself from overusing, "but" you are freer to give constructive critiques. Where possible, eliminating but means you won't say, "But don't throw a high fastball."

Thirteen Ideas for Success in Any Occupation

Even successful people are only successful sometimes. Everyone confronts headwinds occasionally. A baseball player knows he will eventually strike out, fly out, or ground out if he goes to bat enough times. The odds are close to 70% against the batter getting a hit. But if the player can be successful 30 to 33 percent of the time, he can make a lot of money. A professional player doesn't let the 67 to 70% failure rate dominate his thoughts. His only thought is that the next at-bat presents a new opportunity to succeed.

Every worthwhile action carries within it two outcomes: success or failure. Winston Churchill pointed this out when he wrote, "Success is going from failure to failure without loss of enthusiasm." When successful people fail, they learn from the experience and then move on—the wiser—to try again. They don't see failure as a final but as

That Reminds Me of A Story

a learning experience.

Are you looking for ideas that will help you get ahead? Here are 15 ideas you may want to consider that offer guidance for short-term and long-term success.

- Develop a positive—can-do—attitude. A positive attitude generates genuine enthusiasm and is a critical determinant of success.

- The best players usually win. Therefore, invest most of your time and energy in self-development. Be the very best you can be each day.

- Have an innovative spirit. Always look for ways to change and improve everything you do.

- Keep your knowledge current and your skills marketable. The person who continues improving his knowledge and occupation skills will be ready when an opportunity presents itself.

- Align your actions with your mission. Ask, "Does this action take me closer or move me farther away from my goal?"

- Learn to prioritize and do high-return tasks first.

- Act; execute. Good intentions will not get you promoted. Each day, take practical steps to help you achieve your goal.

- Be a problem solver. Evaluate the facts to discover the camouflaged solution hidden within the problem.

- Never lose sight of the goal. Forget the wake, steer the boat, and keep your eye on the goal.

- Identify your core values. These are your "bottom-line" values. You will fight for your core values, which identify what you believe is right, no matter the circumstances.

- Focus on results, not on being busy. Never confuse activity with results.

- Have integrity. Do what you say you are going to do.

- Celebrate and have fun. Successful people balance a strong work ethic with a timely victory reward celebration.

Include these thirteen ideas or principles in your success plan. As you execute your plan, follow the advice of Napoleon Hill, who noted, "Patience, persistence, and perspiration make an unbeatable combination for success."

I Am a Supporter and not a Celebrity.

Celebrities and superstars take a lot of work to meet. I've never crossed paths with Elvis Presley, John Wayne, Billy Graham, Jennifer Aniston, or even Simon Cowell. There is one star I would like to meet. Peyton Manning.

Historically, there are many heroes. Some stand out. Christopher Columbus, Ferdinand Magellan, Martin Luther King, Ponce de Leon, and Jonas Salk are among the standouts. These individuals experienced fame. With a group of committed supporters, these individuals would be prominent.

I realize I am a supporter and not a celebrity. I know I'll never be a star or celebrity when I am honest, and neither will most other people. My support role is to advise, encourage, provide emotional support, motivate, and give reassurance to a friend. A supportive friend isn't focused on themselves. They concentrate on supporting the other person; they deeply care for others. In a supportive role, you show kindness and compassion to someone at a difficult or unhappy time.

Even on the worst days, a supportive friend will be there for you. And you must be there for them.

As a supporter, you show you have more than a bit of a part to play. Whom did you support this week?

Black and White Hands

My cousin, an elementary school teacher, loves her job. She is careful about what she does and says to her students. The children express themselves more freely. Often, their ideas are out of the box and show keen insight.

She tells the following story. The classroom teacher has many responsibilities. I accept that responsibility. I went to school to study and prepare to be an elementary teacher. Each day, I look forward to helping mold the minds of my students.

In college, I posted a saying by Ben Franklin on my corkboard. I aimed to remember. "Involve me, and I learn." My end game was to involve the students in the fundamental points of the learning lesson.

One day, after class was over, I walked one student out. I held the hand of a seven-year-old black student. He said to me, "You and I are different."

I did not prepare for this, but I knew that inevitably, one day, the subject of race would come up. Before I could speak, he said, "Your hands are bigger than my hands."

With that, he ended the discussion.

It's always hard to explain why young people understand the solution and don't even know the problem. We adults see the problem and have no answer.

That Reminds Me of A Story

Instant Charisma

Given the option, most people would choose to be charismatic rather than dull. We prefer to be charming as opposed to unexciting. But you don't have to look far to discover that only some are attractive and appealing. I know people who were born with this seemingly magnetic gift. I know others who have gained it through experience and practice. I know a few individuals who have yet to learn what I am writing about.

There is no magic script to follow to become charismatic; a charismatic person emits a magic spell. Charisma opens doors, secures interviews, boosts sales, improves deals, and ensures preferred seating.

Years ago, I created a product that would have motivational-hungry organizations beating a path to my door. My product is a 4-oz. aerosol can of magic that I named "Instant Charisma." It would be my path to riches. People liked the product. Some wanted a free sample. No one wanted to pay for it.

One day, while trying to help our shy teenage daughter be more extroverted, my wife and I signed her up for a high school speech class. She wasn't happy.

For her first speech, I suggested she take a can of Instant Charisma and show how it helps create a positive environment, assisting others in building confidence, commanding attention, and attracting success—to be winners.

Reluctantly, she took a can to class. When it was her time to present, she walked to the front of the students and asked, "Are you looking for an edge? An advantage? In my hand is a magical 4-oz. Can of Instant Charisma. This personal magic helps you achieve goals and develop self-motivation.

What happened next was magic. Her classmates began clapping and cheering. They loved the concept and passion for her performance. At that moment thirty-five years ago, it changed my daughter's life.

The magic wasn't in the aerosol can but in the clapping. It was evidence of her audience's support, approval, and encouragement. When our daughter exited her cocoon to fly, it was instantly, but not because of Instant Charisma. Her classmate's authentication of her worth transformed her into a beautiful butterfly.

Her mother and I noticed the change immediately. She walked faster, stood taller, and smiled more.

Sometimes, the story is not about you. It's about the other person. Your encouragement and support may help them stand straighter, walk taller, smile more, and take flight. In one minute, you can make someone's day better. Today and every day, tell someone you are proud of them—the power of encouragement releases the power of charisma.

Is Your Work Shift Ever Over?

As I was driving from work to the hospital one day, I was thinking how lucky my friend was to be coming home the next day. His elective procedure and recovery took less than two days. Someone told me the average hospital stay was 4.6 days.

While in my friend's hospital room, I overheard one hospital employee say to a fellow employee, "My work shift will soon be over." Because of her statement's emphatic and defeatist tone, I assumed her work shift had been difficult and tiring. And, in a short time, her shift would be over. Or would it?

While the Dictionary defines "shift" as a scheduled period of work or duty, work can also be a blessing. Just ask someone who is unemployed but looking for work. Question a graduating senior who has yet to find a job. Ask a retiree who retired "too soon." Ask an experienced older adult who feels they face age discrimination. Or ask the employee who is genuinely under-employed and desires to contribute and earn more.

Work is a blessing when viewed as an opportunity. Employment is the chance to show your skills and prove you can handle additional responsibilities. Let people know that your shift never ends.

In the meantime, ask, "What good work can I do on my current shift?"

SECTION 5: THOUGHTS

Stories that come to mind.

Wayne Nalls

The Rain Remembers

I relaxed as I sat in my rocking chair on my front porch last week and enjoyed the late summer rain. The rain provides a spruce-up that a sprinkling system can't match for my yard.

Rain is essential to make contemporary life possible by providing water for agriculture, industry, sanitation, and electrical energy. Without oxygen, we die instantly; dehydration produces the same results without water.

My wife says, "City rain and country rain are different." Country rain has a unique smell and soothing and relaxing sound.

It surprised me to hear a seed farmer say, with a slight glimmer of humor, "The rain remembers." He explained, "I have a 300-acre seed farm that requires much rain. It sometimes rained only on 50 to 100 acres, leaving the other 200 acres dry. But the rain remembers, and when it returns, the other 200 acres (and maybe all 300 acres) will benefit from the falling country rain."

People's lives will be better because the rain remembers.

Dictionaries Define Things, or Do They?

It is time to purchase a new dictionary. I prefer the printed type.

My standby Dictionary, The American College Dictionary,

That Reminds Me of A Story

published in 1959 by Random House of Canada Limited, needs to be updated. It contains all the words I need. It has 1,421 pages, starting with "A" and ending with "Z."

I am not too much for new words when old words work. The problem with my dictionary is that the old familiar words have new meanings. Take "hero," for example. My Dictionary defines a "hero" as "a man of distinguished valor or performance, admired for his noble qualities." These words best describe doctors, nurses, first responders, and Mother Teresa.

Doctors diagnosed Lou Gehrig with (ALS). This incurable disorder forced his retirement at age 36. In his last appearance at Yankee Stadium, this hero said, "I'm the luckiest man on the face of the earth." For me, these are heroes.

But, as I read, watch, or listen to the news, reporters define today's heroes differently. I see or hear descriptions other than people with distinguished courage or noble qualities.

Social media describe today's heroes as overpaid athletes who assault their spouses, engage in rape and murder, celebrities who take off the most clothing, and males who are now females and females who are now males.

No matter who the President is, they will not fit my dictionary definition of a "hero." In the '50s, we described the President as a politician; the same is true today. What we need is a "leader or stateswoman."

I think I'll also keep using my old dictionary.

Possibilities

Have you noticed that people excuse themselves from helping someone in need by placing the individual's demands on them? "If they are hungry, need clothing, sleeping on the street, they should get a job."

It isn't just the down and out; it is every person. With encouragement, we can shake off the situations that limit us.

At age 76, Grandma Moses saw the possibility of being an artist.

At age 39, Martha Stewart saw the possibility of being more than a stockbroker.

At age 24, Stephen King saw the possibility of being more than a janitor and living in a trailer.

At age 30, Harrison Ford saw the possibility of being more than a carpenter.

At age 80, Moses saw the possibility of being a leader with God's encouragement.

That Reminds Me of A Story

At age 31, the Apostle Paul saw the possibility of a changed life.

At 31, St Augustine saw the possibility of being a Christian.

People should look at the situation, see an opportunity, and commit. Even better, understand the possibility of lending an ear; this person could be what God created them to be. When was the last time you saw someone's potential and took the time to encourage them?

Reset Expectations

Blind spots are those things about us that we are unaware of. Discovering our blind spots helps us find our areas for improvement. Discover my blind spots by identifying all the things/events/people that trigger me in a day. I feel annoyed/weird/affected. These represent my blind spots.

Every person has flaws. The most important thing is understanding, acknowledging, and addressing them. Being human, each of us has some false expectations.

Don't expect everyone to read your mind. Many people have a default. Never expect others to know your feelings if you haven't told them. People can't read minds, even if you think they should understand you well enough to decipher your behavior. People's emotional landscapes differ entirely, so don't hold them accountable for your false expectations.

Perfection is not attainable. Stop pretending you must be perfect, and cut yourself some slack. Let go of unrealistic expectations. No one can fulfill everyone's expectations, no matter how hard they try. One can't please everybody, so attempt to accept that and move on!

Be kind to yourself. Once you are more aware, you set high expectations, avoid repeating past mistakes, and make a positive difference with yourself and others.

Setting high standards serves as a useful motivational tool. Expecting yourself to be perfect takes the joy out of life. However, having rational expectations can motivate you to achieve your goals. Transform high expectations into achievable ones and experience less anxiety, depression, and unhappiness.

Make a Difference

"It's easy to make a buck. It's much tougher to make a difference."—Tom Brokaw.

When confronted with an opportunity to make a difference, people often opt out and choose the ordinary. If you want to create a difference, remember Robert Frost's words: "Two roads diverged in a wood, and I took the one less traveled by, and that has made all the difference." Often, the less-traveled road, the less popular position, and the seemingly less rewarding choice will make an extraordinary difference.

Three keys to becoming a Difference Maker:

- Be willing to take risks. Don't allow fear to overcome your desire to make a difference. Anxiety often leads to procrastination. Any action might fail. If you don't try, you guarantee failure. Start doing so, and you can become a difference-maker.

- Be passionate about what you do. A competitive spirit under control can move mountains.

- Commit yourself to what you are doing. Commitment has its foundation in confidence. Confidence plus desire produces steadfastness.

Making a difference is something you can do every day. The old Spanish proverb, "It's not the same to talk of bulls as to be in the bullring," is full of truth. To make a difference, act. It would be best if you got involved. Your goal should be to get into the ring and look for opportunities to create a difference.

Wayne Nalls

The Butterfly Effect

I thought about how much fun I had chasing butterflies as a kid. Butterflies were everywhere, and they were beautiful in color and design. Today, I seldom see butterflies. We should put them on the endangered list.

While living and working in South Florida, I often drove by "Butterfly World." This tourist attraction houses several beautiful gardens and is home to over 20,000 exotic butterflies and unusual birds. People pay $29.95 to view the butterflies, birds, and gardens.

Though I never stopped and toured Butterfly Word, it reminds me of "The Butterfly Effect." This theory says that a butterfly flapping its wings in Peking, China, contributes to the tornado in Lawrence, Kansas. Small causes have significant consequences.

This thought suggests that every person can influence their actions, attitudes, and others' health. If one person can make a difference, can one act also produce a difference? Why not test the idea? Decide each morning for the next week that you will say, "Have a "Blessed Day" or "Thank you" (depending on the situation) to everyone you encounter.

Follow this plan for one week. Address everyone with one of the above statements. You judge if the Butterfly Effect works. When you have a positive (or negative) impact on someone, the chances are that the person will pass it on like a ripple in the lake.

That Reminds Me of A Story

If you only change your life, that counts too.

Whittling

My college student son sat on the bench outside the city library, waiting for it to open. Suddenly, a school bus with 12 to 15 grade-school children arrived on a field trip at the library. Their chaperones told the kids to hold one another's hands, stick together, and not speak to strangers.

As in most small field trips, a young, out-of-the-box boy immediately broke the rules and approached the college student sitting on the bench. One girl shouted to him, "Don't talk to strangers!" The boy thought and then asked the young man on the bench, "Are you a stranger?" "Yes, I am." One chaperone spoke up and reminded the children that not all strangers would harm them.

The boy continued, "Do you have a knife? Strangers have knives, and they hurt kids." The college boy set up straight and said, "Yes, I do, but it isn't for harming kids; I use it for whittling." The boy's next question was, "What's whittling?"

For many people, God is a stranger waiting to hurt or punish them. So, they attempt to avoid Him. But God shouldn't be a stranger; He is your friend and invites you to confide in Him. The Bible says, "Come to Me, all of you who are weary and burdened, and I will give you rest. All of you, take up My yoke and learn from Me because I am gentle and humble in heart, and you will find rest for yourselves. For My yoke is easy, and My burden is light." (Matthew 11:28-30, HCSB)

God doesn't use prayer to punish us but to bless us. If you ask, "Why doesn't God bless me?" You've asked the wrong question.

Parenting

When my wife and I took the children out to eat, we received many compliments from other customers. When we got to our table, we all sat down until we got up to leave. The kids were pleasant to each other and us.

Times have changed, and parental emphasis on manners and social skills has changed. The statistics show that over 185 million children in the U.S. are between six and eleven. Their parents have yet to offer or teach them social skills and manners for many of these children.

My wife and I went to a store to have someone help us with our cell phones. We were sitting at a tabletop waiting. As we paused, two parents became more noticeable — a man with two daughters ages 6 and 8 and a woman with a daughter about seven years old — had lost control of their kids, and the kids were running around the store and shouting at each other. The parents were deaf and blind, or they didn't care. The latter was apparent. You'll see children not in their seats at the table but running around the restaurant, making it hazardous for other patrons and the server staff. Their parents are on their phones or talking, oblivious to the chaos their children are causing.

The Bible says, "Teach a youth about the way he should go; even when he is old, he will not depart from it." (Prov. 22:6, HCSB). This passage reads like a promise to parents who raise their children properly.

This verse warns parents who allow their children to grow up without guidance.

The Buck Stops Here

"For we will all stand before God's judgment seat. So then, each of us will give an account of ourselves to God." (Rom. 14:10, 12, NIV)

Few people accept responsibility for their actions; finger-pointing is the reality. Accepting the blame is taking responsibility, which leads to accountability. Few people and fewer organizations acknowledge that the buck stops with them.

Those who love slogans know a great motto is a nugget of timeless truth. Time resurrects excellent sayings. For example, former U.S.

President Harry S. Truman's motto was: "The Buck Stops Here."

People should accept personal responsibility and quit passing the buck. I believe success or failure measures personal accountability. The more we hold ourselves accountable, the more success we experience; the less we keep ourselves accountable, the less success we have.

Risk avoiders are irresponsible negative thinkers. Successful people are risk-takers and take responsibility for their lives. Practicing personal accountability and accepting responsibility leads to increased self-esteem. You improve your attitude when you assume responsibility for your feelings and thoughts. When you take responsibility for your circumstances, you open the door to new opportunities.

Individuals accept responsibility. It would be better if we acknowledged that the buck stops with me. As the headline states: "The buck stops here." So does this story.

Don't Believe Everything You Read

The word "propaganda" has a foul taste, as does "sour kraut."

According to Merriam-Webster, propaganda spreads information to aid or damage a person or cause. Anyone is a "journalist," extending their thought—whether confirmed—to help their cause or injure

That Reminds Me of A Story

someone else's cause.

While a fantastic technology tool, the computer has clouded credibility, factuality, bias, and reality. Every day, we are exposed to thousands of messages from people attempting to make their reality our reality. The authors established themselves as authentic sources.

Before accepting any statement as correct, ensure it meets these standards:

1. Is the information relevant and essential to me?
2. Is the information complete?
3. Is the source reliable?
4. Is this information verifiable by other sources?
5. Is the information biased?
6. Is the information an attempt to manipulate and motivated only by the writer's self-interest? Beware of manipulation attempts.

Some people like writing and posting and only want to see their thoughts on social media. I get it. I love some of these posts and blogs. However, when the writer claims to have witnessed a three-headed alligator or unequivocally states that humans can fly, this information is not good propaganda.

Information is important. It should be correct and not devalued by people whose only skill is the ability to type.

Advertising sour kraut is good on a hotdog bun is still propaganda.

Two Big Fat Lies We Tell Ourselves

No matter the size of a lie, it's a lie.

While there is only one truth stage, there are three degrees of lying: white lies, fibs, and blatant untruths. The difference between a white lie and a fib is shades of grey. People often cross their fingers as they stretch the falsehood as truth. The difference between a fib and a blatant lie is that a lie deliberately communicates false information.

Faced with a business or career opportunity, people often buy into one of the two biggest self-defeating lies: They convince themselves they are too young to step out or too old to change. As experience proves, either excuse is a big fat lie. The source for both lies in fear. When a person says, "I'm afraid to decide," you're listening to a risk-avoider and a person fearful of success. It's unfortunate, but they will achieve their goal.

The problem with self-lying is that it is easier than lying to others. It is fantastic to complete the delusion that one is too young or old to succeed. People have an alibi: I am too young, or I am too old by not venturing. The purpose of life is to live your dream and help others live their dream.

We waste time avoiding the opportunity when the need for a

decision is evident. In his book "Blink," Malcolm Gladwell writes, "Decisions made quickly can be every bit as good as decisions made cautiously and deliberately." Sometimes, people must accept the challenge and act on the advice of Robin Williams in the movie "Dead Poets Society" "Carpe diem. Seize the day. Make your lives extraordinary." It's hard to understand why more people don't put the "extra" in extraordinary.

I'm not young and don't consider myself too old, so I ate an extra biscuit for breakfast this morning. Consuming the other biscuit isn't part of my dieting program, but it was good. So rather than lie to me, I fibbed.

Where Did the Positive News Go?

Viewing the nightly news is like swallowing poison and waiting for the information to become positive.

The news invites you to tune into the gloom, doom, and despair and includes six free commercials. If you take this, you may experience side effects, nausea, breathing problems, diarrhea, and even death. This reaction happens in 30 minutes and is guaranteed to work for 24 hours.

In its proper state, the news is to inform us. We may not like what we see or hear, but everyday events are expected, and that's not news. The idea of a bank having a typical day of depositing money, cashing checks, and transferring money is not news. A robbery at the bank is news. People going about their everyday lives, working, caring for others, and being role models are not news. Politicians who steal, cheat, and accept bribes are news. An old saying is that a dog biting a man isn't news, but a man biting a dog is news.

A steady dose of negativity creates a negative mind. Is asking the networks to proportion their newscast with 70% negative news and 30% positive too much? I want to see and hear more "good neighbor" news.

Teamwork vs. Kamikaze Recklessness

The Merriam-Webster's Collegiate Dictionary defines teamwork as "work done by several associates with each doing a part but all subordinating personal prominence to the efficiency of the whole."

The saying, "There is no 'I' in the word team," reflects the part of the definition that says all subordinating personal prominence to the efficiency of the whole. Considering this, we should remember that "the whole is greater than the sum of the parts." When cooperating or working together, the team can produce a result that no individual can create.

The "lone wolf" versus the pack concept reminds me of the Japanese

That Reminds Me of A Story

kamikaze pilots of the Second World War who made suicidal crash attacks upon warships. No matter how dedicated and willing these pilots were to fight—exchanging their lives in a single act of dive-bombing their plane onto a ship—their reckless act bore little fruit.

A picture of the success spectrum finds teamwork at one end and kamikaze recklessness at the other. By focusing on team success, we subordinate Kamikaze's desire for personal prominence to cooperation. Nothing beats people working together for a common cause.

Mark chapter 2 gives an excellent example of teamwork. Four men, determined to bring their paralytic friend to Jesus hoping to heal, did what one of them couldn't individually.

1. The men knew of Jesus' healing power and believed He would heal him if they could only get their friend into Jesus' presence. (Verse 3)
2. Each man shared a corner of the mat. (Verse 3)
3. They didn't let obstacles deter them; they were determined and showed remarkable ingenuity. "Since they could not bring their friend to Jesus because of the crowd, they removed the roof above where He was. And when the carriers had broken through, they lowered the stretcher on which the person with paralysis was lying." (Verse 4)
4. Jesus rewarded the faith of the four men. "Seeing their faith,

Jesus told the paralytic, Son, your sins are forgiven." (Verse 5) Then, Jesus said, "I tell you: get up, pick up your stretcher, and go home." (Verse 11)

5. The result of teamwork. "Immediately, he got up, picked up the stretcher, and went out in front of everyone. As a result, they were all astounded having never seen anything like this!'" (Verse 11)

We must bring **people** to Jesus, all people to Jesus, **by all means.**

Choose the Coach Over the Team

In accepting a job offer, people look for salary, benefits, location, company standing in the marketplace, company history, and the people they will work with. While all these perks are significant, we must weigh each to our goal.

The most critical and often overlooked thing is your coach, to whom you will report. People have been brain-washed with the team concept and being a part of a team, and they miss the critical issue—who is the team coach?

Five-star high school football athletes choose the University of Alabama not because it's in Tuscaloosa, Alabama, or because the university is 100 years old. They don't select the Tide because they want to play on a team with skilled players because of the nine national championships or the 22 SEC titles. They chose Alabama because they wanted to be coached by the best college football coach in America, Lou Saban.

Life offers two head coaches: Jesus Christ and Satan. Both coaches have large teams, and each team member plays for the coach of their choice.

Scripture states that two coaches can't coach a player. "No man can serve two masters: either he will hate one and love the other, or he will hold to one and despise the other. Ye cannot serve God and mammon." (Matthew 6:24, ASV)

Coach Satan offers wealth, prestige, and a life of ease. Coach Jesus' promises are in the book of Matthew. "So don't worry, saying, 'What will we eat?' or 'What will we drink?' or 'What will we wear?' The idolaters eagerly seek all these things; your heavenly Father knows you need them. But seek the kingdom of God and His righteousness first, and all these things will be provided for you. (Matthew 6:31-33)

They offer athletes scholarships to attend a specific university. Most scholarships are the same, but the head coach is unique. The athletic rewards vary. The Bible comments on the proper reward of choosing Jesus as your coach. "For the wages of sin is death, but the gift of God is eternal life in Christ Jesus our Lord." (Romans 6:23)

When you select a coach, choose the best. Choose Jesus.

Wayne Nalls

The Art of the Handwritten Letter

There is something unique about a handwritten personal letter. It's better than an email, no matter what the social media gurus claim. We read emails and often delete them. An excellent handwritten note can last a lifetime and become a treasured possession.

Letters celebrating my graduation and scholarship are precious to me. Other treasures include an invitation to my wedding and several thank-you letters from former associates who said they enjoyed working with me.

A personal handwritten letter tells you a lot about the writer. When you open the envelope, you unmask the sender. You quickly determine the writer's mood and sincerity. Is this a giving letter providing information, a compliment, or an offer letter requiring something?

The time of the handwritten letter is about to pass. Teachers teach cursive writing to a few people in school. Some people don't take the time to be personal; they zip off a cold email and hope they won't offend.

Over the years, I have saved many treasured handwritten letters. Today, I deleted yesterday's emails.

That Reminds Me of A Story

My Name Isn't on A $50 Bill. But It's on My Credit Card

If a field of study creates a few millionaires, "anthroponomy" is one. I have not met an anthroponomical practitioner. But I know a person's name is significant and has the power to shape and influence their life.

Knowing your name allows a business to personalize the seller/buyer relationship. Personalization occurs in several ways. Understanding your customers' buying habits and addressing the customer by name are only two critical ways.

Recently, I made a reservation with a local car dealer to have my car serviced on a Friday morning at 9:00. I showed up at 8:55. My motto (borrowed from the Army) is: To be early is to be on time; to be on time is to be late, and to be late is non-acceptable."

The service representative greeted me with, "How can I help? WOW! How can I help? Really?" You have a computer that shows I will be here at 9:00 a.m. with my 2015 car for the 12,000-mile service and updating two recall notices.

I'm sitting in my 2015 silver Ford Escape, looking at you. It's 8:55 a.m. If you had glanced at your daily schedule, you would know who I am and why I am here. A great greeting would have been, "Good morning, Mr. Nalls. I see you're right on time, and we're ready to update those two recalls and service your Escape."

What makes this a great greeting?

1. The greeting, "Good Morning," is upbeat and friendly.
2. Using my name tells me you know who I am as a person and not just a customer.
3. "I see you're right on time," acknowledges my punctuality, and tells me you appreciate me being on time.
4. "We're ready" signals that you expect me, and the service will be prompt.

You know my VIN but not my name. Like most people, my name is important to me, and when someone uses it, it helps bridge the gap between us. If you're in business and I'm buying your product or services, calling me by name sounds like a relationship.

While my photo isn't on my credit cards, they all have my name. I handed my card to a cashier, and they scanned it and handed it back, along with the receipt. I say, "Thank you," and they wait on the following customer. They had my credit card with my name and never once stated, "Thank you, Mr. Nalls. We appreciate your business."

I had my computer serviced yesterday. The company does the repair using the internet to "look" at my computer. Once they determine the problem, they fix it. This morning, I got up, and the new router they had connected for me wasn't working. I called them. Before I explained my problem, I said, I'm sorry to have to call you back, but." The service tech interrupted me and stated, "No, Mr. Nalls, you don't need to apologize. YOU ARE THE REASON I HAVE A JOB"! "Names have power." —Rick Riordan, American author.

Ten Tips for Living a Happy Life from a Backyard Gardner

Ten steps to backyard gardening and you can apply actions to live a fulfilled and fruitful life.

1. PREPARE THE GARDENING SITE. Thorough preparation precedes accomplishments that give happiness.
2. READ THE PLANTING DIRECTIONS ON THE SEED LABEL. A well-conceived set of directions for achieving personal happiness comprises two major components—your attitude toward life and others.
3. WEEDS AUTOMATICALLY GROW; YOU MUST CARE FOR VEGETABLES. Don't defy this quirk of nature. Pull the weeds and use the time to think about friendships that may need a little extra attention. Successful associations depend on the removal of unwanted distractions and complications.
4. DON'T FORGET THE FERTILIZER. Plants need nutrients. Do everything possible to strengthen your tomorrow. Enthusiasm, like fertilizer, is worthless left in the container. Spreading it will help.

5. DON'T EXPECT THE SEED PLANTED TODAY TO BURST OUT TOMORROW. Growth is a process. Imagine the frustration and disappointment if you only think of the present. There is a future, and the reward of our efforts today comes with it.
6. THE SEED YOU PLANT IS THE CROP YOU HARVEST. Carrots produce carrots, and radishes produce radishes. Many people need to connect what they do with what they get.
7. SMALL SEEDS CAN PRODUCE A LARGE CROP. Small incremental actions can form the basis of significant results.
8. GARDENING DOESN'T TAKE MUCH TIME, AND THE BENEFITS ARE WELL WORTH THE EFFORT. "A garden," wrote Gertrude Jekyll, "is a grand teacher. It teaches patience and careful watchfulness, industry and thrift, and, above all, trust."
9. USE PLANT MARKERS SO YOU'LL ALWAYS KNOW WHAT YOU PLANTED. Happiness begins with short-term goals to measure progress. Without markers to guide, there is a tendency to wander from the plan. As with vegetables, you don't want to be surprised by the outcome.
10. GET GROWING. Execution is the key to success in gardening and living a happy life. As we practice these ten keys, good things happen.

That Reminds Me of A Story

Fourteen Ideas for Success in Any Occupation

How you respond to failure determines your odds of success. Every worthwhile action carries within it two potential outcomes: success or failure. Your response to failure (and you will sometimes fail) determines whether you will be successful. Winston Churchill pointed this out when he wrote, "Success is going from failure to failure without loss of enthusiasm." When successful people fail, they learn from the experience and then move on—the wiser—to try again. They don't see failure as final. But as a learning experience.

Are you looking for ideas that will help you get ahead? Here are 14 ideas that offer guidance for short-term and long-term success.

- Develop a positive—can-do—attitude. Without this, there is no success. A positive attitude generates genuine enthusiasm and is a critical determinant of success.
- The best players usually win. Therefore, invest most of your time and energy in self-development.
- Have an innovative spirit. Always look for ways to change and improve everything you do. Searching for "ways" opens you to new and better ideas.
- Keep your knowledge current and your skills marketable. The person who improves his knowledge and occupation skills will be ready when an opportunity arises.
- Looking back may be the best way to get ahead. If you are

not on track, look around. Determine where you deviated from your plan. It is often not a significant change that you make, but a relatively small shift can lead to missing the primary target. Correct your errors and move forward.

- Align your actions with your mission. Ask, "Does this action take me closer or move me farther away from my goal?"
- Learn to prioritize and do high-return tasks first.
- Act; execute. Good intentions won't get promotions. We pay people to get results. Each day, take practical steps that help you achieve your goal.
- Be a problem solver. Evaluate the facts to discover the camouflaged solution hidden within the problem. Find new and better ways to do your work.
- Identify your core values. These are your "bottom line" values. They identify what you believe is right, no matter the circumstances.
- Focus on results, not on being busy. Develop the ability to get things done to achieve goals. Never confuse activity with results.

Have integrity. Organizations look for commitment and follow-through. Do what you say you will do. Accept responsibility and accountability for your actions.

- See the Big Picture. Success is a journey, never a destination. View your current position from a big-picture perspective.

- Celebrate and have fun. Many successful people balance a strong work ethic with a timely victory celebration.

Include these ideas or principles in your success plan. As you execute your plan, follow the advice of Napoleon Hill, who noted, "Patience, persistence, and perspiration make an unbeatable combination for success."

Exploring the World Beyond Your Comfort Zone

Some people, like Marco Polo, Christopher Columbus, Isaac Newton, Jonas Salk, and Neil Armstrong, left the familiar to learn about the unfamiliar.

Twenty years from now, you will be more disappointed by the size of your comfort zone than the size of the area you could have explored. To remove the boundaries, you must enter new paradigms.

What did Sir Isaac Newton mean when he stated, "I do not know what I may appear to the world, but myself, I seem to have been only like a boy playing on the seashore and diverting myself in now and then finding a smoother pebble or a prettier shell than ordinary, whilst the great ocean of truth lay all undiscovered before me." Newton meant he regarded himself as only living in his small area while others explored new areas. That insight remains valid.

You may never experience time travel, living on other planets, discovering a cure for cancer, etc., but we can make many uncharted discoveries outside our comfort zone. Attempting something new offers new experiences, thoughts, tolerances, friendships, and fresh adventures.

Don't let the comfort of your present zone restrict you from experiencing the great ocean of opportunity lying all undiscovered before you.

Six Thoughts on Success

The key to success is self-improvement. Investing in your education can help you ensure success. The importance of education continues to grow as more and more people realize that their education will determine their professional and personal success.

1. No one sets out to be a failure. People have talked about being lawyers, doctors, teachers, and sportswriters, but no one says, "I want to be a failure."
2. People need a personal success goal and a plan for achieving it. The individual must define the dream and commit it to paper or a computer.
3. It doesn't matter where you start, but you must begin. I have found that successful people take positive action every day, bringing them closer to goal achievement.
4. Celebrate. The best celebration is to share what you are

learning with someone else.
5. Never get mad at someone for being more successful than you. It is not their fault.
6. Study what others have worked hard to gain, learn, and swiftly apply their knowledge, not wasting valuable time re-inventing the wheel.

Some researchers find a To-Do List of up to six tasks best. The goal is to complete the activities on the list. The strategy is to accomplish the things on your to-do list each day. Without a list, you can't establish priorities. You get the first project done with a list and then move on to the next focus. You may not accomplish all six goals but will complete the higher-priority projects.

Someone said, "You always have time for things you put first."

A Steal at a Yard Sale

I found—two books by Benjamin Hoff at a yard sale. The books initially sold for $15.00 each, but I bought both for $1. Paying fifty cents for each book means I saved $29.00. Originally published 40 years ago, "Tao of Pooh" and "The Te of Piglet" are classics.

While reading the first book, I discovered the story of the Uncarved Block and was hooked. "The essence is that things in their original simplicity contain their natural power, which is easily spoiled and lost when that simplicity is changed. When you discard arrogance, complexity, and a few other things that get in the way, eventually, you discover that simple, childlike secret known to those of the Uncarved Block: Life is fun."

Reading "Tao of Pooh" reminded me of a wise proverb. "What we think, we become." So, think positively, and you can't think negatively. Think negatively, and you can't think positively. The essence of a happy life is being positive rather than negative. Like the lesson of the Uncarved Block, a proverb reveals a simple natural truth. You will always move toward your currently dominant thoughts.

SECTION 6:
THE VALUE OF TIME

The statute of limitations never expires on stories about the value of time.

The First Activity of the Day

Everyone has the first activity of the day. The important thing is not that we all start our day with some action but that the event sets the stage for a happy and prosperous day. After brushing my teeth, I have breakfast: one sweet roll, a slice of cranberry-walnut bread covered with peanut butter, and black coffee. I have the same breakfast most mornings.

The smell, taste, and touch of the roll, the toast, and the coffee make me happy. I don't get distracted by checking emails, reading a newspaper, listening to the radio, or viewing the TV. I concentrate on the roll, the bread, and the coffee. The hot coffee awakens me, the sweet role stimulates me, and the peanut butter toast provides a "delight for the morning."

You may start the day with a hot or cold shower to invigorate you. The sound and feel of the water "raining" on your body may be your first activity. Some people's first action includes a devotional Bible study and prayer time. They meditate on what they are thankful for and lift others through intercessory prayer.

For some productive people, exercise is the first morning activity, including jogging or walking. These events can lead to optimizing and maximizing the rest of the day. The isolation of running or walking provides a sense of nature. Once we finish exercising, we are better prepared to engage in the day's opportunities.

That Reminds Me of A Story

These are four key elements of the FIRST ACTIVITY OF THE DAY.

1. It's a ritual. You do it every morning at the same time and place. Do this, and you develop a habit of success and happiness.
2. Live in the moment. Isolate your thinking to the present moment. Don't focus on yesterday or tomorrow—enjoy the now. Living in the moment creates energy and enthusiasm for the day.
3. Enjoy and expect. Look forward to enjoying coffee, jogging, meditation, the shower, or whatever you define as your *First Activity of The Day*. You're in your "zone," own it.
4. It's a positive activity that increases self-esteem. You set the stage for the rest of your day in these first few minutes.

After completing the FIRST ACTIVITY OF THE DAY, consider how you want the day to end—what will success be? Then, from that success point, look back to the present and decide what you must do to achieve your goal.

The possibilities are unlimited when you launch the day your way! I know a cup of black coffee, a sweet roll, and a slice of cranberry-walnut bread topped with peanut butter give me more good mornings and productive days than I deserve.

Wayne Nalls

Some Things Are Just Worth the Time

Time means different things.

For the eight-year-old child who just celebrated Thanksgiving, Christmas is a long time in the future; for the parent, the 33 days represent a short time for gift buying. To the employee looking forward to the weekend, Friday can be a long time away. For a manager with a report due, Friday is a drop-dead deadline. For an engaged girl, her marriage day can be a million hours away; for the bride's father, the time has flown, and his little girl will be gone too quickly.

What intrigues us about time? Time has no past or future. Time is about the present. George Harrison said of time, "It's here now that's important. There's no past, and there's no future. Time is a very tricky thing. All there is the present. We can gain experience from the past, but we can't relive it, and we can hope for the future, but we don't know if there is one."

It may be time to heed Mitch Albom's words: "It's such a shame to waste time. We always think we have so much of it." We may have less time than we suppose. Therefore, we must use the time to improve ourselves and help others.

Your age, sex, nationality, education level, or how much wealth you have doesn't influence the speed of time. Maybe C.S. Lewis was thinking the same way when he wrote, "The future is something which everyone reaches at the rate of 60 minutes an hour, whatever he does, whoever he is."

As you think about time, consider whether any of the action steps listed below are worth your time. It Is Time To:

- Ask, "Can I help?"
- Inquire about another's opinion.
- Show appreciation.
- Thank someone for helping make you a better person.
- Realize the only time you have is the present.
- Send a thank you note.
- Listen more than you talk.
- Review your personal goals and self-improvement plan.
- Eat at a new restaurant.
- Celebrate!

The purpose of using time isn't just to use it. It is to utilize it wisely. Engage in activities that are important to you or positively impact others.

We are not here to mark time. Our purpose is to make time valuable for ourselves and others. When time ends, your legacy will be all that remains.

Wayne Nalls

How Did it Get So Late So Soon?

Today, because I have more years behind me than before, I appreciate and understand the great truth presented by Dr. Seuss: "How did it get so late so soon? It's night before it's afternoon. December is here before it's June. My goodness, how the time has flown. How did it get so late so soon?"

Because time is finite and opportunities are limitless, successful people choose and invest in priority projects and activities. The most critical projects deserve our best attention. Use time working on tasks that bring you closer to your goals and eliminate distancing activities that sap strength. Avoid the "Everything is important" trap. Everything is not essential. Only the truly important is vital. Unsuccessful people choose the default choice and buy into the comfortable, non-important, not urgent activities – though they may be fun.

"We measure real-time with clocks and calendars. Yet, our sense of time may be short or long. Our lives are enhanced, or limited, by the personal management of two critical factors: Time and Money. We have some influence on both outcomes, yet elements beyond our control direct them-" It would help if you guarded your time because once it's flown, it's gone.

One day, you will say, "How did it get so late so soon?" Let Dr. Seuss' statement challenge and motivate you to use your time skillfully. Yes, be busy, but make it a focused busyness. Hold to your plan and do activities that lead to goal achievement.

A Time to Let Go

There's a story about the defining moment when a father and son must let each other grow. The father took his 10-year-old son, a Boy Scout, to the boy's first Boy Scout weekend camp-out.

The son wanted to earn Scouting's highest rank, Eagle Scout, which was one step on his journey. Future actions would include service, community engagement, and leadership development.

The scout learned to set up his tent at camp, build a fire, and tie rope knots. The most permanent lessons about life came from his scout manual or scout leader and his interaction with his dad.

The camp-out was a two-night adventure, and the father dropped his son off on Friday and told him he would return on Saturday to see how things were going. He returned midday on Saturday and was surprised to see his son doing well. The son showed him the most enormous can of peanut butter the father had ever witnessed. Then, he showed him his campsite and introduced him to the troop leaders.

It was soon time for the father to leave, and the son walked with him to the car. The father told him he would return to pick him up on

Sunday afternoon. Suddenly, the boy started crying and asked his father to take him with him. "I want to go with you, Dad. Please take me home."

"No, son, you must complete the camp, and I will pick you up on Sunday." The son turned, still crying, and walked back toward the camp. The father also turned and strode to his car, thankful his son could not see him weeping. That day, the father learned a life lesson: he had to let go so the son could grow.

I am that father, and my son grew to become a father. Someday, he will have to let his daughter succeed.

See The End of The Day in The Start of The Day

The best time to plan your day is early morning when your mind is fresh, unencumbered, and open to creative thought. This time is "Contemplative Time"—a time to contemplate how you choose to end your day and what actions you will take to ensure success. AM reflective Time is about turning what you need to do today into the PM things you've done.

Reflective time is an invitation to achieve your goals, reduce stress, and live a happier life. This 15-minute morning session won't supply you with something you don't have. Instead, it unleashes what already exists in you and unlocks your potential. During the reflective time, you aim to look at the day ahead and ensure you will do what you must.

There is nothing like a pending deadline to sharpen a person's focus.

A news reporter must get his or her story written by the deadline if he or she hopes to see their article in the paper or on the newscast. It would help if they did only things related to completing the story.

You know how you want the day to end. This guides you to do those things that help you achieve that end and not do things that have no bearing on goal achievement. If you complete the day as you designed it, you must make every action bring you closer to your goal.

Here are five benefits you can expect by predetermining your day.

1. Seeing the end of the day at the start of the day enables you to develop a plan for getting things done.
2. In determining daily goals, you discover ways to achieve them.
3. It helps avoid the "activity trap" and encourages you to work today only on those activities that connect you to your goals.
4. Achieving today's goals motivates tomorrow's tasks.
5. Life is more exciting and rewarding when you live today as planned instead of waiting to be surprised.

Start today with a vision of how you want your day to end. List what you must do to achieve that ending, and do what you must do so the day concludes as you designed it.

We Know So Little

My wife wanted a lemon tree for her birthday. I bought her one that looked healthy and was the right size—3 feet tall. I repotted the small tree in a larger pot and placed it on the pool deck. Everything was fine. The wife loved the tree, and in four months, the tree was budding. The only problem was that some leaves turned yellow and fell off the plant. We expected yellow lemons, not yellow leaves.

Yellow lemon tree leaves alert that something is wrong. I spoke with a salesperson at Ace Hardware and explained my problem. The salesperson diagnosed the leaf problem—yellow leaves, either too much water or not enough. The salesperson felt the leave and said, "It's dry and brittle. Your plant needs water." His answer was critical knowledge that I did not have. On the way home, I thought about how much knowledge and little time I had to tap into even a tiny part.

That Reminds Me of A Story

Time Another Success Dimension

"Time is free, but it's priceless. You can't own it, but you can use it. You can't keep it, but you can spend it. Once you've lost it, you can never get it back."— Harvey Mackay.

A pet idea of mine is that people should be born with all the wealth they will ever have, and as they age, they correspond less and less. When life finally ended, their bank account would be down to zero. It is nice to envisage having your wealth when you can most enjoy it. But life is not designed that way. We spend our lifetime gaining possessions, and then most people end life with a little something to pass on to the next generation or the government.

We possess all our time at birth and then lose it as we age until we die. The second is the most valuable and fleeting of the two. As author Denis Waitley wrote, "Time is the most precious element of human existence." While time is valuable, it is not infinite. Its value comes from its scarcity and its fleetness. John Randolph stated, "Time is always the most valuable and perishable of all our possessions."

Time has a dimension of speed. Calculate the rate by the number of candles on the birthday cake. When we are young, time drags; when we are old, time flies. You never ask a youngster if they have a minute; they have a lifetime. Ask an older adult if they have a minute, and they may answer, "That's all the time I have, a minute."

People have more gadgets to create time but experience information overload and extra activities.

There are many thoughts on time. Here are some that are worth your time.

- Take care of your minutes, and the hours will take care of themselves. — Lord Chesterfield

- The time is always right to do what is right. — Martin Luther King, Jr.

- One always has time enough if one will apply it well. — Goethe

- The bad news is that time flies. The good news is that you're the pilot. — Michael Altshuler

- In truth, people can make time for what they choose to do; it is not the time but the will that is lacking. — Sir John Lubbock

If I had to choose my favorite, I'd pick the quote by Martin Luther King, Jr. If we take the time to do what is right, we rightly invest where the payoff is the largest.

We inversely relate the importance of a project to the time available; the more important the project, the less time available; the less critical the project, the longer the time available. The best people should always work on the priority project. Invest time where there is a big payoff. I find I can't do everything. My experience leads me to believe that some things are not worth the time.

Successful people are those who have mastered time. They know that time has no past, no future, only a present. You can't change the past, nor can you predict the future. But you can make the best use of the moment.

We should not be so busy living that we cannot make a life. Each 24-hour period contains great possibilities and corresponding significant responsibilities. Search for opportunities to create a life while earning a living. It may be your time.

We all come into the world without wealth but arrive on time, within our allotted time. As we age, we gain wealth but exhaust our time until there is no time. There are no resets or carry-over minutes. Zig Ziglar wisely stated, "Remember, you can earn more money, but when time is spent, it is gone forever."

SECTION 7:
FOOD FOR THE SOUL
Stories that make the mouth water.

That Reminds Me of A Story

Hoecake and Michelangelo

After pouring in the oil, my mother heated her small iron skillet. When the heat was proper, she poured the cornbread batter, and hoecake bread appeared in two or three minutes. The thin, six-inch round bread was crisp and tasty, mostly the circle's outer three inches, which was extra fried and crispy. My mother served me a bowl of turnip greens. No one makes hoecakes like my mother.

When I finish serving my wife's potato salad, I say, "Ho mangeao bene," the phrase Michelangelo used to describe his mother's meals — "I have eaten well."

The food may have been too good for me. At eighty, I still eat like a twenty-eight-year-old man, but I don't exercise like an eighty-year-old man. Too large an amount of food (or activity) can be harmful. However, excellent food is the exception.

I do not know your favorite dish or who prepares it. It may be your wife, grandmother, aunt, or someone else. Whatever the plate, I am sure you can say, "Ho mangeao bene."

The Disappearing Pie

I heard the story of a pastor and one of his associate pastors who visited the home of an elderly church member. The lady, who had been a church member for 20 years, was under the weather and was excited about the home visit.

After updating the pastors on her health and recent activities, she insisted on serving homemade squash pie. The two pastors were not among the squash pie lovers, but not wishing to offend their parishioner, they took the pie's slice when offered. The pie had a strange odor, and the prospects of this pie sampling were not what either pastor wanted.

The senior pastor wolfed the pie and secretly prayed to God, "If I get it down, Lord, please keep it down." He looked at the other pastor, and his pie dish was empty. How did he swallow the pie so fast? The pastor thought. He couldn't have eaten it and must have put it in the flowerpot beside him.

Before they left, they prayed with the lady and quickly departed. Once outside, the senior pastor asked what he had done with the pie, afraid he had placed it in the flowerpot and the lady would soon notice it.

The second pastor said, "I couldn't eat the pie, so I slipped it into my inside coat pocket. I figured cleaning the coat was cheaper than going to the ER."

That Reminds Me of A Story

Snickers

Kids love to eat candy for breakfast, lunch, dinner, and in-between meals.

I love Snickers; they aren't on my diet plan. But how can you turn down a candy bar crammed with peanuts, caramel, and nougat coated with milk chocolate? The right candy bar can help you maintain your weight; it may benefit you by adding extra pounds to assist you in staying warm.

As a child, my parents only allowed small amounts of candy. When given the opportunity, I chose Snickers. A mix of Snickers and Coke-Cola is the original energy-boosting combo.

Our brains cannot remember certain things: our fifth-grade classmates' names and the gift we received on our second birthday. But we recognize the taste of foods, especially Snickers. I love winners, and Snickers is the world's best-selling candy bar.

Peanut Butter

I eat a lot of peanut butter on sandwiches, Ritz crackers, and sometimes with a slice of pineapple. Eating peanuts and peanut butter helps control hunger without leading to weight gain. It is high in valuable nutrition and fiber.

There are many ways to eat peanut butter; the best approach is to consume a peanut butter and grape jelly sandwich. There are many peanut butter brands: Peter Pan, Jif, Skippy, and Smucker's, to name a few. My favorite is Jif peanut butter. I have a 16-oz. jar in my pantry.

While my father was in the Army, my mother, brother, and I stayed with our paternal grandparents. They had a farm in South Georgia and grew peanuts, among other crops. I used to watch Papa plant his peanuts and then harvest them. I still see him following his mule and the cutting plow from morning until night. He couldn't afford fertilizer, so the harvest was slim. He waited for the rain and prayed for a good harvest. Sometimes, he had peanuts to sell; other times, he planted, and the rain did not come, so he had to wait another year.

We celebrate George Washington Carver as the "Peanut Wizard." He was a world-famous chemist whose research on peanuts, sweet potatoes, and other products helped poor Southern farmers vary their crops and improve their diets. He discovered over 300 uses for peanuts, including chili sauce, shampoo, shaving cream, and glue.

George Washington Carver developed hundreds of products using peanuts. But not peanut butter.

That Reminds Me of A Story

Second Chance

I am thinking about my lunch today of andouille-crusted grouper.

You do not order dessert after eating this blackened grouper fillet crusted with a blend of panko breadcrumbs, creamy parmesan cheese, and finely diced Cajun sausage. I even think dessert is insulting to the meal and the chef.

We used to dine at this restaurant several times a month. Then, two years ago, we invited friends to join us for dinner and enjoy the superb seafood. Going from top-grade food to bottom disaster food should be illegal. Our meals were late, the entrée was cold, and the food was tasteless. Nothing was good except for the tea.

Today, we gave them a second chance, and they rewarded us with the meal I described above.

I don't know a better way to summarize this article than to quote Anurag Prakash Ray, "A second chance means nothing if you didn't learn from your first."

Defining Moments

I enjoy a few pleasures more than eating my wife's potato salad. When consumed, I say, "Ho mangiato bene" (I have dined well).

She goes the extra mile to prepare the mixture of boiled potatoes, onion, celery, eggs, and radishes. Her salad is no "get-by" potato salad; this is the extra-mile salad. She brings out the best in her salads and people.

By doing the unexpected, Jesus turned water into wine. Mary washed Jesus' feet by going beyond what was required. By going the extra mile, Jesus forgave Peter for his denial. The four friends clung to the ropes, exceeding everyone's expectations as they lowered their paralytic friend through the roof so Jesus could heal him.

Each person has an opportunity to exceed their best. What are the moments that define you?

Oreo Cookies

I sampled a new Oreo cookie—Oreo Thins with lemon flavor cream. Nabisco's manufacturer describes these new cookies as "thin & crispy sandwich cookies." The small print in the Nutrition Facts box states that four new sandwich cookies contain 150 calories.

It's funny about food and calories. Foods with a high-calorie count taste better than foods with a low-calorie count. Milkshakes taste better than a glass of milk. The original Double Stuffed Oreo — a chocolate sandwich cookie with two chocolate wafers and a sweet cream filling- is better than the new Oreo Thins.

That Reminds Me of A Story

When I was a kid, my mother rewarded my brother and me with a glass of cold milk. We dunked the Oreo cookie in cold milk and ate it. That's still my favorite way to eat Oreos. We also parted the two wafers, ate the cream, and then ate the crackers.

I chose the original Oreo over the new Oreo Thins.

Over the last 104 years, kids and adults have enjoyed this classic cookie manufactured at the Nabisco factory in New York City. Initially, the manufacturer released two flavors, the original Oreos and a lemon meringue flavor, which was discontinued in 1920.

Classic cookies are addictive. They are reintroducing the lemon-filled cookie, which could be classier. My son, John-Carl, introduced his year-old daughter to Oreos, the originals. I bet it's her favorite cookie now and throughout her life.

Now and then, the new beats the old; this is not the case with the new Oreos.

I Smell Ice Cream

The top five ice cream flavors for US adults are chocolate, vanilla, strawberry, mint chocolate chip, and butter pecan. History records that the first ice cream flavor was Alexander the Great's ice concoction, mixed with honey and nectar. Since 1660, ice cream has been a popular dessert for the public.

I stayed with my granny and papa on their farm in Brinson, GA, during the 1940s. One of my best food memories is hand-churned vanilla ice cream.

Papa hooked up the two mules to his wagon and set out for a small general store to purchase a 25-pound block of ice for making homemade ice cream. They carefully wrapped the ice in a Crocker sack to keep it cold. He couldn't afford to do this often, and the round trip was a little over two miles. The mules ambled, and the round trip took about two hours.

Granny poured the ice cream mix into the churn, and Papa placed the chopped ice in the churn. We all churned the ice cream mix to keep it moving while it froze. And I never considered it work because I knew turning the handle meant I would soon eat a dish of ice cream.

In 1999, my wife and I took our first grandchild, Michaela, to The Mall of Georgia; she was two years old. While we shopped, Michaela fussed. To quiet her, I promised I would buy her some ice cream. I forgot the promised ice cream as we exited the mall, but my granddaughter had not. As we headed to the car, she said, "I smell Ice cream."

Suddenly, I smelled it, too.

That Reminds Me of A Story

My Wife's Soup

My mother's chicken noodle soup was great for a cold or a sore throat. My wife's excellent vegetable beef soup is made by boiling beef and various vegetables in water; it tastes and smells healthy. There isn't a specific recipe—a little of this and some of that. A bowl of her soup ignites every taste bud in my mouth.

Scripture tells the story of a tired and frustrated Esau selling his birthright to Jacob for bread and a hot bowl of vegetable and meat soup. In doing so, Esau showed how little he cared about his rights as the firstborn son. (Story in Genesis 25:29-34 ICB)

Don't let your tiredness and frustration dictate your actions, which will affect your joy. Be sure you don't sell your soul for a cup of soup—even if it is my wife's soup.

Dinner on the Grounds

Sundays at church are the best, especially when there is a worship service and a potluck dinner. The potluck dinner is a way of socializing, allowing both men and women to converse and enabling the children to play together.

My mother's secret for a successful dinner on the grounds was to get my young brother and me our meal and seat us out of the flow of traffic. This arrangement worked until one Sunday; she placed us under the dining table with our dinner and a Coca-Cola.

The dinner tablecloths hung over the side of the table, hiding us from the adults passing down the line choosing their food. Everything was fine until my brother and I shook the Coke bottles with our thumbs over the top opening. Quickly, the cola fizzed, and we spewed the foam everywhere.

Ladies began to scream and jump around. The fizz from under the table caught them by surprise. My mother diagnosed the problem quickly. She ripped the tablecloth up, revealing that my brother and I were shaking the cola bottle and smiling.

We did not smile long.

That Sunday, I learned that things do not go better when you shake up a Coca-Cola bottle and spew it indiscriminately.

Today Was a Good Day for a Hamburger

My wife, nephew, and I drove to a local place for hamburgers. As always, the hamburgers were excellent.

After eating, I dumped our plates and napkins. On the way back to my table, I witnessed the rude action of one of the restaurant's employees. As I passed the drink bar, there were six people around

That Reminds Me of A Story

it. Two were refilling their drinks; two were waiting to fill their cups. Next, a senior couple in their late 80s attempted to exit the building through the tiny aisle. Both had drinks in their shaking hands. The gentleman walked with a cane.

Suddenly, one employee hopped between the four people on the left side of the small aisle and me on the right, hell-bent on picking up his next order. He barely missed hitting the older couple and dashed on. We avoided a disaster. I waited thirty seconds, and as the server returned, I told him how rude he was. His only reply was, "I didn't see them standing there." He lied, or he was blind.

The second event I observed was a lesson in ownership. I saw a young man in his early 30s busing and rearranging the chairs at three tables opposite me. He cleaned the tables and rearranged the 12 chairs—four at each table. Stepping back to observe his work, he saw something he did not like. He mixed the chairs. His action said I must set the chairs right.

Thinking he might be a manager, I asked if he was. No, he said, "I am the owner."

Today was a good day for a hamburger. It was also an excellent day to see why a person earns $12 an hour and why someone else earns six figures a year.

Wayne Nalls

The Thanksgiving Meal

I've always preferred Thanksgiving over Halloween. Miniature Hershey Bars, Babe Ruth, and Tootsie Rolls stuffed into a trick-or-trick bag do not compare to turkey, dressing, gravy, and cranberry sauce on the family table.

The Plymouth colonists and the Wampanoag Tribe shared a feast in 1621, now remembered as one of the first Thanksgiving celebrations.

Turkey, potatoes, stuffing, canned pumpkin, and other staples have increased in price this year. The U.S. government estimates food prices will be up 9.5% to 10.5% this year; historically, they've risen only 2% annually. We often worry about the calorie count in a Thanksgiving meal, according to estimates by the Calorie Control Council. Americans take in 3,000 to 4,500 calories at their Thanksgiving celebrations.

We all need something to be thankful for, and this year, on November 24, 2022, let us be grateful for our Thanksgiving meal, be it turkey, ham, chicken, or fish. You can exchange your meal for a peanut and jelly sandwich with only 300 calories. But remember, you will need to eat something else to maintain your daily calorie needs — 2,000 calories a day for women and 2,500 for men.

Prices are up, and the bird supplies are down slightly, but one meal can get our daily collection of calories. We can be thankful; we still have food, family, friends, and a primarily optimistic future, among other blessings.

SECTION 8:
PERSONAL STORIES

Unique stories that prove life is fantastic.

That Reminds Me of A Story

Halt. Who is There?

I attended my required ROTC summer camp at the University of Florida between my junior and senior years. Many other cadets did not enjoy camp time. I did. It was a time of firsts. I shot my first rifle, flew in a helicopter, threw a grenade, and learned to use a compass.

Guard duty was an activity I did not enjoy. This action occurred after nightfall, a time to be in bed, not out walking the camp's perimeter. My job was to look for an unidentified person or party and require them to halt and be identified.

The idea is to challenge any suspicious activity. My duty was winding down when I noticed a hunched-down object about 30 feet away staring at me. I was told that one of the regular officers would test the cadets for their alertness. So, I said, "Halt. Who goes there?" No answer came forth, so I repeated my command and moved closer to investigate the intruder, only to discover my intruder was a fireplug.

When I arrive at the pearly gates, I hope to hear, "Advance, well done thy good and faithful servant and not, 'Halt. Who is there?'"

Pennies

This morning, I stooped and picked up a penny from the Dunkin Doughnut parking lot. It wasn't a nickel, dime, or quarter, just one penny.

Though the penny coin is 0.75 inches in diameter and 0.0598 inches in thickness, I still stopped and picked one up from the sidewalk or floor. Benjamin Franklin's words still ring true, "A penny saved is a penny earned."

Like most people, you have a jar of pennies around the house somewhere gathering dust. It's not like you set out to be in the business of penny storage, but they've just accumulated.

The U.S. Mint's 2017 coin production figures show that its two coin-producing factories in Philadelphia and Denver produced over 8 billion pennies for the year.

If you were to put $.01 in a jar today, then each day after that, you place the same penny amount as the day it is. Compounding your penny savings would give you $667.95 by the end of the year. The most you would ever have to drop into the jar is $3.65 on the last day.

Okay, now, a penny for your thoughts: If your church has a fund-raising goal and you have 200 members, this penny-a-day program would raise $133,590 by the end of one year. Now, that's some fund-raising dollars. A penny saved is a debt paid.

Twice I Met the Governor

I have had two occasions where my first perception of a person was negative, and then I found something good about the person.

Lester Maddox served as the 75th Governor of the U.S. state of Georgia from 1967 to 1971. Having garnered national attention in 1964 for refusing to serve African Americans at his Pickwick Restaurant, noted for his folksy manner, he proved a moderate governor and implemented many African American policies. While accompanying my wife to the hospital to visit one of her co-workers one night, I sat in the ER room lobby. It surprised me with 12 African Americans when, at 10:30 pm, Governor Maddox, accompanied by two Georgia Highway patrolmen, entered the room. He smiled and shook hands with everyone in the room.

The African Americans smiled, stood, and shook his hand. Some said, "Welcome, Governor!" All were aware of who he was, and it pleased them that the Governor took the time to visit with them while they waited for their loved ones.

The second time I met the Governor was during the final exam for one of my graduate marketing courses at Georgia State University in Atlanta. One of my fellow students spent most of his course time arguing with Dr. David Schwartz (author of The Magic of Thinking Big), and he knew he had to do some big thinking for his final report.

The classroom door opened when his report was due, and Governor Lester Maddox arrived with the State patrolmen. The student introduced the Governor and said Maddox would present his final oral exam, "Marketing and Government."

At the end of this high-profile presentation, Dr. Schwartz said, "This is what I'm talking about when I say, 'Think BIG!'"

Angels in the Neighborhood

I grew up in a neighborhood comprising ten families and twelve kids. It was a classic 50s environment. We had paved roads, but the driveways were dirt-filled and great for shooting marbles.

Everyone knew everyone. We didn't lock the house doors and often left the car keys in the car. We traded comics, collected sports cards, and swung on a big Crocker sack swing. Kids had free range of the neighborhood, and we were in and out of most homes daily.

Any parent could discipline any child if engaged in non-safe activity like tackling football. The problem with neighbors punishing you was usually a two-for-one. When you got home, your parents disciplined you. The police did not patrol the neighborhood, and no crime-watch signs were posted. The fathers and mothers were the first responders, and my mother was head of the swat team.

Often, we had neighborhood cookouts. Several men would go fishing and fry the fish they caught in an iron cooking pot filled with boiling grease. The mothers provided grits, hush puppies, slaw, drinks, and desserts. Our angels became chefs and cooks, and the kids were the servers and members of the trash detail.

I compare the camaraderie and the combined parent discipline team with today's neighborhood, where many people don't know the people next door. We all need neighborhood togetherness and parent angels that provide love, discipline, role models, and safety.

While I continued to Type

My mother insisted I take a typing course in my senior year at Ocala High School. The typing class was not "cool." Typing, like shorthand, was for girls. My mother discounted that thinking, and I enrolled in a typing class.

My fingers are short, and I remember the keyboard being complex. I still find the QWERTY keyboard a mystery. The frequently used pairs of typebars were separated so as not to clash and get stuck at the printing point, and my typing style allowed for typebar clashing.

When we had a typing test, the teacher, Ms. Emma Smith, timed you for five minutes — it seemed like five hours.

Ms. Smith gave the start command to type. I remember the clanging sound of the keys hitting against the platen and then the sound of someone beating the carriage return lever, and I started typing again.

The other students hit the return bar more often than I did, and I heard their key taps. I was not too fond of typing, not the sounds of the keys typing or the sound of the return bars. It was the sound of silence while I continued to type.

Expect Obstacles

In 2017, I attended a high school graduation held in a small town with a population of around 7,000—there were 110 graduates. I, along with 1,500 relatives and friends, enjoyed the ceremony. It began by presenting the United States flag and a lone trumpeter playing the Star-Spangled Banner. Then, with a hand placed over our hearts, we recited the Pledge of Allegiance. That's when I became emotional.

Fifty-eight years ago, I attended high school graduation mine. The ceremony was in a small town. The event was in our school auditorium; tonight's graduation was on a football field.

That Reminds Me of A Story

Apart from special church services and Eagle Scout Ceremonies, I rarely stand with a group of people with our hands over our hearts, reciting the Pledge and listening to the national anthem. I attend very few sports events, so I am not in the stadium or the arena when this moving experience happens.

I'm offended and upset when people don't stand during the playing or singing of our National Anthem and don't place their hands over their hearts. On Memorial Day, I am emotionally confident and express my patriotic feelings. I remember the many servicemen and women who gave their lives so that we might become residents of the greatest country in the world.

The graduates will learn that their education isn't complete; it has only begun. As one young speaker said, "Expect obstacles. It's not the 'setbacks' that count but the 'comebacks' that decide our success."

My First Day on the Job

I arrived early for my first day on the job. Things could have gone better. As I sat in the big Sears parking lot, I waited for other employees to arrive to see where you entered the building. Once inside, I observed the other employees go to a time clock and "punch in." So, I found my timecard and punched it in.

Wayne Nalls

They hired me as a salesperson in the Farm and Fence department, so I went there. No one else was there, so I spent the next five minutes looking at the products in my department. Suddenly, two more people joined me and introduced themselves as coworkers.

When the first customer arrived, I approached him, introduced myself, and asked, "How can I help you?" In a college sales course, I learned that the customer was interested more in how I could assist them than in what I knew, which was very little.

Once we found the product he was looking for, we headed to the cash register, where one of the other sales associates offered to ring up the sales. I was thankful, as I had no cash register training. The additional sales assistants were helpful all day in ringing up my sales. It wasn't until the following day, when my department manager asked me why I had no sales, that I realized the other sales associates had not helped me; they had allowed themselves to my sales by ringing up the transactions using their numbers, not mine.

I did not know the location where I needed to take a bio-break on that first day; I did not know the restroom's location. I had to ask.

The first day on the job went differently than planned. But I learned things that would serve me later when I hired people. I told new hires how to get into the building and instructed them on using the time clock and the cash register.

That Reminds Me of A Story

The best thing I told them was the location of the restrooms.

Supporting Role

I was sitting around and thinking and realized I had never met a celebrity. I never crossed paths with Elvis Presley, John Wayne, Billy Graham, Jennifer Aniston, or Tom Harmon. One star I would like to meet is Peyton Manning.

If you look at history, some heroes stand out. On his four voyages across the Atlantic Ocean, Christopher Columbus began the European colonialism era in the Americas. Ferdinand Magellan sailed around the world, and Ponce de Leon discovered Florida.

While these famous people experienced fame, they would not have been prominent without a supporting team. A quote says, "It takes a village to raise a child." It takes a group of committed supporters to make a person famous.

Every so often, I realize I am a supporter and not a celebrity. I know I'll never be a star when I am honest. My goal is to find someone worthy of support, and my role is to support them.

I Like to Remember, But I Don't

Some people have the gift of good remembrance; I don't. I am forgetful.

As I age, I encounter the problem of forgetfulness; I lose my keys, glasses, cell phone, and many other things. I had them, put them down, and now I can't remember where I last had them when I needed them.

I was thinking about ways to help me remember the items I put down. Just imagine being able to find your car keys when you need them. My idea is to have a "Lost & Found" table in one room of my house. Anytime I place a thing down, I put it on the table. Therefore, when I need an unavailable item, I go to my lost and found table and retrieve it.

I don't know whether this idea is new. The idea of tables is not. The history of tables traces its history back to the 7th Century B.C. Maybe someone who reads this will tell me if my idea has a previous patent.

Now, if I could only remember where I placed my lost and found table, I would retrieve my keys and go for a ride.

A Powerful Black and White Teaching Moment

Of all the things I could write about, I chose to write about an event I witnessed fifty-seven years ago during the summer ROTC camp at

That Reminds Me of A Story

Fort Benning, GA.

Our regular Army company commander—a Captain—had other duties one day. His replacement was a black captain; this incident occurred years before "African American" became the correct description.

In our first company formation with the new captain, all 200 white and Hispanic cadets stood at attention while he walked down the cadets' line. Each time the captain turned and faced a cadet, the cadet saluted; the captain returned the salute. People know that a junior officer salutes a superior.

All followed the rules and regulations until the captain faced the white cadet on my left. The cadet said he could not salute a black man, so the captain ordered a chair brought out of our barracks to him.

What happened next was an exceptional training moment. The captain calmly removed his jacket — the one with ribbons and medals on it, including the two silver bars insignia rank — and neatly draped it on the chair. Then, he stepped back and faced the offending cadet. "Son," he said, "I'm not asking you to respect me. The United States Army is not asking you to respect me. Congress, the American people's representative, tells you to respect me based on the commission they gave me."

"Now, Cadet, you salute the uniform and the power the uniform represents, not the individual who wears it." Without hesitation, the cadet saluted the jacket draped over the chair. The captain returned the salute, reached over, took his coat, and put it on. Then, he smartly moved on down the row.

Fire in the Dorm

It sometimes seems like memories fade, and a special one reappears. One of those reappearing memories occurred when I was a junior at the University of Florida.

Students often wonder what possession they would save in a dorm fire. Would it be their television, computer, clothes, or other cherished possessions?

On December 12, 1961, I chose my most treasured possession: me. While I studied in my room in Murphree G dorm on the second floor of the building, I had only one stairway and an outside door for each section.

While studying, I heard someone yell, "Fire, fire!" The fire alarm, invented in 1890, didn't ring because there wasn't a fire alarm in the hall. The smoke alarm didn't sound because battery-operated smoke alarms weren't available until 1969. But the voice warning dates to creation.

That Reminds Me of A Story

The fire, which started in a first-floor room, quickly filled the section with dense smoke, making exiting by the only stairway impossible.

The fire caught me by surprise before I could leave by the stairway. I opened my door and found the hallway filled with thick smoke. I didn't want to grope down the stairs, so I closed the door, tied some sheets together, and climbed out the window.

The university newspaper, the Florida Alligator, ran a story about me escaping a fire by tying sheets together and climbing out the window.

I'm holding on to that memory and thinking about the safety of the present dorm residents. I was lucky. According to FEMA, about 3,800 university housing fires occur yearly in the United States. When students face a dorm fire today, I hope they are as lucky as I was in 1961.

If someone were to ask me today what possessions I would save in a home fire, they would be my wife and two children.

What is the Next Million Dollar Idea?

I collect many old things, including old newspaper clippings, because I find essential information in the articles.

Nearly every senior recognizes the phrases "Walk the Dog" and

"Around the World." As a kid, I used to sit in the movie theater and watch Duncan's men display their dazzling skills with yo-yos. Skateboarding, Frisbee, Hula Hoop, Slinky, Ant Farm with Ants, and Galicia Ice were just a few of the fads I enjoyed during my childhood.

The classic was the Pet Rock. When he got a brilliant idea, Gary Dahl, an unemployed copywriter, would sell a rock for $4.95, even though his friends told him it was the stupidest plan they'd ever heard. Nobody was going to pay for something you could find in your backyard. Dahl sold over a million rocks, including the pet rock I bought.

I had to have the latest fad, whether Rickie Tickie Stickers or Rubik's Cubes, because all the other kids had one.

Personal Introductions

Some people have the natural gift of introducing a friend, family member, work associate, or manager. "Jake, please meet my wife, Suzi. Suzi, this is Jake Smith. Bill, this is Mr. Jones, the President of my company. Mr. Jones, this is my friend Bill Williams." The introduction is simple.

Other people feel awkward making introductions. They are often nervous and may forget one attendee's name. I've attended company functions and witnessed many coworkers never introduce their spouse or significant other. Maybe they forget or don't care to make the introduction.

Personal introductions, when done right, can be memorable. I recall an unforgettable introduction for my son, an Army Captain stationed at the Pentagon in Washington. He worked for the Deputy Secretary of Defense, Dr. Paul Wolfowitz. Frequently, he accompanied Dr. Wolfowitz to the White House for meetings. On one trip, he realized they were in the reception area outside the Oval Office. Dr. Wolfowitz asked the receptionist if "He" was in. She answered, "Yes," but Condoleezza Rice was speaking with him. The "He" and "him" referred to then-President George W. Bush.

After a few minutes, the receptionist told Dr. Wolfowitz that the President would see him. Dr. Wolfowitz opened the door and walked into the Oval Office. My son sat down and studied the surroundings. But for only a minute. Dr. Wolfowitz opened the door and said to my son, "The President wants to meet you." Think about that for a moment. Lay aside your political leanings and think about a 28-year-old Army Captain from Dallas, Texas, meeting the United States president.

The President didn't start the introduction; it was Dr. Wolfowitz. He knew the effect that meeting and being introduced to the President would have on the young captain. The three spent several minutes talking, and then the President invited the two men to accompany him to a briefing. Cool stuff. No, the takeaway from this story is that the Deputy Secretary of Defense took the time to introduce an Army Captain to his Commander and Chief.

Some people are too busy, and others make time for introductions. It comes down to priorities.

One Sunday and Six Saturdays

For fifty years, I looked forward to retiring. I thought about all the things I would do: sleep late, read exhaustedly, write a book, experience the good times, and most of all, enjoy the freedom to do as I pleased.

During the 18,250 days I worked, I looked forward to vacations and days off. I welcomed three-day weekends. If you set out to describe a promising work career, you'd describe mine- or I would, anyway.

My advertising, sales, and marketing jobs used the creative right side of my brain. I was fascinated that 1 + 1 equals 2 or 11.

I had the privilege of associating with many creative people, including Dr. David Schwartz, author of the mega-selling book The Magic of Thinking Big, Charlie Clark, Professor of Senior education and training consultant at the Goodrich Institute for Personnel

That Reminds Me of A Story

Development at Kent State University, and Mike Vance, former director of people development for Walt Disney Productions, Disneyland, and Walt Disney World. Mike popularized the phrase "Think Out of the Box."

Suppose it sounds as if I'm describing a mythical "perfect" career. I am, but it's my actual career of 50 years.

As much as I liked this career, I looked forward to the day I retired. The day came, and I quickly discovered an actual retirement week: one Sunday and six Saturdays. I should have considered the Saturdays and worked a couple more years while making retirement plans.

A Canadian Visit Memory

While living in Akron, OH, our family took two trips to Canada. On the second trip, we visited Niagara Falls, one of the most famous waterfalls globally. Our first trip was to Kitchener, Ontario.

We prepared for our first international trip with our driver's licenses, birth certificates, social security numbers, marriage certificates, and a mailing envelope showing our home address.

My wife was driving when we arrived at the Canadian border crossing. When it was our turn to cross, the border guard asked,

"Citizenship?" Suzanne answered, "No, thank you." The guard again questioned, "Citizenship?" For the second time, my wife replied, "No, thank you."

Then we realized the border guard was asking where our citizenship was. Did we want to become Canadian citizens?

A Senior Moment

I am old enough to retire, young enough to enjoy what the other retirees say.

Senior living apartment complexes provide endless stories. You must listen and observe what's going on around you. For example, last night, management said the cleaning crew would clean the carpets in our four-level building. The notice also told the residents of the time of the two elevator carpet cleanings.

There needed to be more than just posting the cleaning times for one of the grey-haired ladies. As she and I stood reading the note, she asked, "I wonder when they will clean the elevators on my floor?"

Rich Man, Poor Boy

When I was a kid in Florida, television was new. My family didn't own a TV, and we didn't know anyone who did. In the early black-

and-white days, the kids in our neighborhood only dreamed of what we would see if we had a TV.

One day, I discovered I could send two Wheaties labels to Battle Creek, MI, and they would send me a personal TV. I never went through two boxes of cereal so fast. I mailed two labels to Battle Creek, and in two weeks, I received my TV. The package was too small to be my awaited gift. Eagerly opening the box, I discovered a 2-inch by two-inch "TV." The directions read, "Place the small circle of exposed film in the back of the unit and look at the wonder of nature." What I had was a mini version of a view master.

One day, I saw a TV antenna installed on a neighbor's house, only five doors from mine. The other neighborhood kids joined me as we stood in the street outside of the "rich man's" house. It was a unique and wonderful sight to see this tall antenna, including guide wires, being installed. The 2-man crew strapped the unit to the chimney of the house.

The installation crew finished their job and drove away. I stayed looking at the house and its new TV antenna. I stood for 10 to 15-minutes, but no one invited me to see their new TV, the first one in the neighborhood.

Months later, when my father's boss invited us to his house to see The Lone Ranger on his 12-inch black-and-white round screen, I saw my first TV program and TV set. Strangely, I always assumed the setting for The Lone Ranger was Texas, and there was snow all over the screen. At that moment, I heard the word "static" for the first time. We were 90 miles from the broadcasting station and received interference (snow) on the screen. The snow didn't bother me. I was in a rich man's home, experiencing TV for the first time.

A Doctor, a Carpenter, and a Realtor

Often, it takes time to meet a classy individual. This week was the time. I met three professional Christian men: a doctor, a carpenter, and a realtor.

The doctor and I exchanged biblical stories and his spiritual journey during the exam. There is a Bible study room in his house. He is a proactive witness and prays for his patients, neighbors, and the lost. He got his current position with my primary doctor's practice because my primary and he are Christians. This doctor is a man who walks his talk.

The second classy man I met was a professional carpenter. I'm moving and need several fix-up projects before listing my house for sale. My elegant, professional realtor is a notable Christian who recommended the carpenter. You did not ask, but I encourage you to pray for the realtor's wife, who is facing a bone marrow transplant, to fight her cancer. She has an exact match, her sister.

That Reminds Me of A Story

From the start, this carpenter's spiritual viewpoint was clear. He said he was a believer and hoped I was, too. During the three hours he worked on the first day, he shared spiritual stories of witnessing and helping people experiencing homelessness.

We remember it is natural for people to resist meeting new people because they fear they won't like them and the meeting will be unpleasant. It is better to expect to meet a few classy individuals than to avoid people unlike you. You may encounter a professional like a doctor, carpenter, or realtor who loves the Lord.

Sometimes, Before You Ask, You Know the Answer

I asked, "Are you a Christian?" She said, "Yes." Before I asked the question, I knew the answer. Then why ask?

The cashier line at the restaurant where my wife and I had just eaten was short. As I waited to pay the bill, only one person was ahead of me. There were two cashiers, one training the other. It surprised me when the trainer asked me for my ticket before the young African American lady ahead of me had completed her transaction. When the lady walked away, I stepped up to pay my bill. My second surprise happened when the cashier said, "You owe nothing." Yes, the 20-something lady ahead of me paid my twenty-five-dollar dinner bill.

When I realized what had happened, I hurried out of the restaurant, looking for my benefactor. Only one car was backing out of its parking space. I approached the driver's side to thank her for her thoughtfulness. After saying, "Thank you," I asked her, are you a Christian? She stated, "Yes." I knew the answer before asking the question.

Today, I saw hope for America in the form of a young African American lady and an 80-year-old Caucasian male, one receiving a blessing and the other being blessed.

A Moving Staircase

When I was very young, I experienced my first ride on an escalator in Rich's department store in Atlanta, Georgia. Even though I had ridden a passenger elevator several years earlier, I stood in awe as I watched this moving staircase carry people between Rich's floors.

I stepped onto the escalator and rode to the next floor. Once there, I got on the down escalator and returned to the first floor. I repeated the process several times. I know people who fear riding escalators, and like every other fear, it has a name: escalaphobia.

Today, people may be confident about stepping on a moving staircase but fear it. Here is a short list of fears. There are many more.

That Reminds Me of A Story

1. The fear of poverty

2. The fear of failure (Atychiphobia)

3. The fear of death (Thanatophobia)

4. The fear of enclosed spaces (Claustrophobia)

5. The fear of developing a disease (Nosopho)

Scripture verses can comfort you when you face fears.

God has not given us a spirit of fear and timidity but of power, love, and self-discipline (2 Timothy 1:7)

I am with you, so do not fear. I will strengthen and help you; I will uphold you with my righteous right hand (Isaiah 41:10)

Even though I walk through the darkest valley, I will fear no evil, for you are with me; your rod and staff comfort me. (Psalm 23:4)

Don't experience Godophobia. Step on the moving stairways and be ready to meet God on the next level.

I've Walked This Road Before

Albert Einstein said insanity "is doing the same thing repeatedly and expecting a different result." This definition reminds me of the 1993 movie Groundhog Day, where a Pittsburgh weather reporter is stuck repeating the same day in a small town.

People make the same mistakes repeatedly and expect different results. Use the mistakes as tactical points for improvement.

Keys for exchanging your Groundhog Day with a new day are:

Create your day. Don't let the past dictate your present. Enjoying life is about what you do, not what you have done. Lay out a plan and stick to it.

Replace your negative habits. Replace a bad habit with a habit that is more productive for you. Apply your positive attitude to the new day against your former negative attitude. Repeating positive habits replaces negative habits. Be an artist. Paint your canvas as you want it. Every day starts with a new canvas. You choose the paints, brushes, and subject.

Combine an attitude of what I can do with a sense of urgency. It is easy to talk about a new day but challenging to live it. Get up in the morning eager for success and the new day because today you will act.

As Einstein famously stated, "We cannot solve our problems with the same thinking we used when we created them." Don't just continue to walk the same road; it will lead to frustration. Replace negative habits with positive ones and travel on an alternative route.

That Reminds Me of A Story

Sometimes, a Dog is Not Man's Best Friend

A friend of mine was dating a cute young lady, and he wanted to impress her. The lady said she was going away for the weekend and needed someone to sit her dog, a miniature dachshund. My friend did not like the dog's excessive barking, and the dog did not like my friend. And his girlfriend knew this. Hoping to impress his girlfriend, he volunteered to keep the dog.

The weekend was a trying time for my friend and the dog. The dog spent his time yapping and nipping at the ankles of his volunteer house sitter. My friend tried to avoid the dog and spent his time cleaning and straightening up his girlfriend's apartment.

On Sunday afternoon, about two hours before the lady returned, my friend placed a couple of pots and pans in the cabinet above the stove. The dog came into the kitchen and grabbed the bottom of his slacks. Startled, my friend turned around and dropped a large iron frying pan that he held onto the dog, killing him.

When the girlfriend arrived home and discovered her dead dog, her boyfriend explained what had happened. The distraught girl seemed to accept his story. But two weeks later, they were no longer seeing each other.

Sometimes, a dog isn't a man's best friend.

Yes Ma'am

When our family lived in Chicago, my wife was a home mom who cared for our two children, a daughter and a son. This was our first time living outside the South; we had never experienced snow.

My wife had trouble grocery shopping because we had only one car, and I used it to go to work. By the time I got home, it was after six o'clock. When we lived in Chicago, you could not purchase beef after 5:00. It was a rule in all the grocery stores. At five, an employee covered all the meat with a white cloth, signaling no more beef purchases.

One mid-morning, my wife took our kids to visit a lady friend. The lady asked the kids if they wanted a cookie during the conversation. Our two-year-old daughter answered, "Yep!" Quickly, my wife asked Natalie what you are supposed to say. She said, "Yes, ma'am."

The friend offering the cookies said, "We don't say, 'yes ma'am and no ma'am here in the north.'" My wife corrected her by stating, "We are not planning on staying here long, and when the kids go back to the south, they must know how to say, 'yes ma'am' and 'no ma'am.'"

It seems we have lost a bit of courtesy, and many kids aren't being taught manners at home. Parents can't expect schoolteachers to fill the void. Teaching good manners is an opportunity to help your children learn to respect and be responsible.

Prince to Pauper

Now that I am in my early eighties, I think about when I was a young father. Fatherhood (or motherhood) is not a title given to you but earned through the trials and the good and bad experiences that mold a parent.

One of my experiences was a difficult transformational lesson. I was in my living room, relaxing and talking with my son, when my daughter came in and said, "The car is down the road with a flat tire." She said nothing else as she ascended the stairs to her bedroom, where she entered the room and closed the door.

Taking my son with me, I went to change her tire and bring the car home. When we arrived, my daughter was still in her bedroom, with a closed door. I did not go up to talk with her. Her teenage hormones were working overtime, and I knew a discussion would soon be an argument. No parent has won a debate with their teenager.

As I think about the incident, I realize that day, I went from being a prince to a pauper. Before the flat tire incident, I could do no wrong in my daughter's eyes. She would slide in between my wife and me when we ate dinner. Wherever we went, she would hold my hand, laugh, and look at me with Google eyes. Things changed in our relationship. She had become a woman, and I remained her dad.

Sixth Birthday

It was at least one month before my sixth birthday. I told my mother and father I wanted a pony for my birthday. I had never had a dog and didn't want a cat as a pet. I promised to take care of the horse. I had chosen a name for him, Tema.

As my birthday drew nearer, I reaffirmed my desire for a pony. My parents would ask if there was something else I wanted. "No, I told them."

On February 8, 1946, they surprised me with a small, gift-wrapped box on the dinner table and a cake topped with six candles. There was no pony in the room. I blew out the candles and opened the gift. Inside was a six-inch high plastic pony.

The story of King Midas and his wish that everything he touched would turn into gold is an example of letting our wants exceed our needs. Once his wish was granted, Midas quickly realized his wish was not a blessing but a curse. Everything the King touched turned to gold.

The moral of this story is that you should not be greedy and want more than you need. Think deeply before making choices; each has consequences, so make wise choices. Appreciate what you already have, no matter if it is a small plastic pony.

The Over Night Tan Man

Although you didn't ask for my advice, people seldom do. Here's something to keep in mind. There is no overnight tan.

You'd have to be of a certain age to remember the vintage Coppertone ad featuring the little three-year-old child who gets her pants pulled down by the Cocker Spaniel. The Coppertone tan product helps you go from pale to tan.

When I think about the Coppertone ad, I remember my overnight attempt to become a tan man. The event took place in my sophomore year of college. I was and am a fair-skinned person. All my attempts at becoming a bronze god were to no avail. I bought a product, Man Tan, applied the lotion one night and expected a gorgeous and authentic bronze man when I woke up the following day. I was so excited about my transformation from pale man to bronze man that I got up several times at night to check my progress. I saw none.

The morning came, and I rushed to the mirror to see only a streaked orange face and arms. I looked horrible. There was no stunning man in the mirror looking at me. Touted as an overnight-developing sunless tanner lotion, it became an overnight, orange-streaked disaster.

I quickly attempted to wash the orange look off. Then I scrubbed, to no avail. Looking back, I should have followed the directions and tested a small area of my body to see how it worked.

I am old enough, 84, to remember the ads for Man Tan and Coppertone and their claims, "Tan Don't Burn Use Coppertone" and "Sleep While You Tan." I used both products but never got a long-term tan or an overnight bronze. I'm still pale, but hopefully, I've gained some wisdom — read the instructions before using any product.

Collateral

The dictionary on my desk defines collateral as providing something as collateral (to get the cash you need for a loan). The list includes a house, land, car, boat, and so forth — really, any tangible assets a lender will hold.

A short distance, three to four miles from our Ohio home, was a shopping mall. The tenants included Sears, JCPenney, and a large mall food court. Hotdogs, hamburgers, fries, and pizza. The food was excellent, but the smell was like a county fair.

That Reminds Me of A Story

On the way from the mall, I saw a service station that had gas on sale at a reasonable price. While we didn't need gas, I stopped and filled up. After pumping the gas, I went inside to pay. The operator's words startled me, "We only take cash!" No problem. I reached into my pocket for the ten-dollar bill—no, ten.

We faced a dilemma without cash, and the station operator refused to take a credit card. He would not let us drive away with a promise to return. I looked at my wife, and she glanced at me. We needed to provide something as collateral to get the cash we needed. She proposed that she remain at the gas station while I returned to the mall and used our ATM card to obtain the ten dollars.

That's what we did. The owner let me drive away if my wife sat in the station.

The ATM popped out the ten dollars. I returned to the station and reclaimed my wife. We agreed to carry cash and not use her as security again. While collateral can include a house, car, boat, and so forth, it doesn't include my wife.

My Favorite Writer

Andy Rooney is my favorite writer of all time. I have enjoyed his syndicated newspaper columns, best-selling books, and three-minute commentaries on the CBS television program 60 Minutes for over a decade.

Andy was the quintessential curmudgeon.

Rooney's sense of humor, sarcasm, and ability to select the most ordinary subjects — toilet paper, the key to the city, small talk at parties, and where time magically transforms them into beautiful stories that captivate his millions of followers.

I recently read an article where the writer listed some of his favorite Rooneyisms. These are also a few of mine.

- Being kind is more important than being right.

- Every politician should be hooked up to a lie-decorator machine when speaking.

- Ignoring the facts does not change the facts.

- That life is like a roll of toilet paper. The closer it gets to the end, the faster it goes.

- Sometimes, all a person needs is a hand to hold.

- That the best classroom in the world is at the feet of an older person.

For a proper ending for this article, I believe Andy Rooney would write, "I know you didn't ask, but here are some thoughts to mull over."

That Reminds Me of A Story

The Realtor Who Helped Us in Need

We bought a house in Dallas, Texas, in 1985, two years before the big housing recession of the 80s. We bought during a time of prosperity. However, our mortgage rate was high. Then, the housing market crashed in Dallas, where we lived.

Experts should have predicted the coming rise in interest rates, the increase in oil prices, high levels of debt, and problems in the banking industry.

The economic conditions hit everywhere. But they were extra hard in Dallas, and when I lost my job, we had to sell our house in an almost non-existent housing market. Over 18 months passed, and no offers. And the bills continued coming.

When our savings account and 10 percent CDs were gone, and we faced bankruptcy, our realtor counseled us not to do it. She said, "I am going to sell your house." After we explained that my wife's paycheck and my unemployment earnings could not cover the mortgage payment and buy groceries, she said, "I will sell your house, and I am confident I will do it in the next 60 days. I am loaning you $5,000 at no interest." We told her we could not accept her gracious offer. Our realtor said, "You will get my loan offer, which will be interest-free.

We accepted her loan on the condition that we would reimburse her for the interest she lost by taking the money out of her personal savings account. She agreed. We sold the house in 50 days. We repaid the loan plus the interest we promised.

S.E. Hinton, an American writer, was right when she wrote. "If you have two friends in your lifetime, you're lucky. If you have one good friend, you're more than lucky."

In selling our house, we discovered that our realtor was more than a realtor. She was a good friend. We'll always be grateful to Dottie for helping us; a friend in need is a friend indeed!

Bingo B 22

I don't know if you played bingo recently. In this 100 percent card game, a winning card is entirely luck. There are approximately 60 million bingo players in the United States, and women play the game more often.

The typical bingo card is flat cardboard or paper with 25 squares arranged in a 5x5 grid. Each space in the grid contains a number, except the middle square, designated a "free" space.

My wife suggested that our eleven-year-old daughter broaden her experiences by volunteering at a nearby senior citizen home. Natalie called the home and inquired about volunteering. The activities director said, "Yes, you can call the weekly bingo game."

The director instructed Natalie to play the game at the center and deal with the other players who were impaired. She suggested Natalie get up close to the woman's ear and say the called numbers forcefully.

When Natalie called the first number, B 22, she raised her voice and spoke into the lady's right ear. The elderly lady responded, "Not that ear, the other ear!"

The room erupted with laughter. It has always amazed me that laughter has a positive or negative effect. The laughter that produces embarrassment is negative. Encouraging laughter is positive.

With Bingo, there's no way to make a losing card into a winning one. With our daughter, there was no way to turn a lousy volunteering experience into a second experience. Volunteering is over. She doesn't want ever to hear someone say, "Bingo."

Three Speeches

Our president made the announcement, assuring us our company had been bought and instructing us not to worry. He was still in charge. One colleague said, "That's speech number one." I thought briefly about his comment.

Two weeks later, there was another employee meeting, and our president announced that the company had received financial aid from our new owners, but he was in charge. Again, my colleague told me, "That speech was the president's final. He won't be at announcement three."

My coworker, the mystic, was right. At our third meeting, they introduced us to our new president, a turnaround artist who would take our organization in disrepair and repair, yielding a hefty profit.

Six months later, we again heard speech number one.

SECTION 9:
OBSERVATIONS I'VE MADE

Seeing stories in daily life

Wayne Nalls

Observations from the Sidewalk

Everyone should take the ride I made this afternoon. The ride was a 20-minute journey to my doctor's appointment. I observed people alongside the road (my wife was driving). She drives better than I do.

You learn a lot just by observing. People were waiting at the bus stops, biking, and walking on the sidewalk, a few looking confused. But what caught my eye and tugged at my heart was the vast number of homeless and dropouts.

You can witness this in almost every city. I felt pain for the individuals and guilt for my country. I saw a pool of potential producers that society has written off.

I saw a man holding a sign, "Hungry, please help." (I wondered if this man could be an entrepreneur if given a chance). I watched a man selling water for $1.00 (given a chance, would this man be a sales manager?) I saw a woman holding a sign, "Hungry, God Bless." (Could she, given a chance, be a dental hygienist?) Next, a gruff man was sharing his little food with his dog. Inside this man, is there a philanthropist given a chance who would help many other people in need, even donate to the construction of a hospital?

America and American businesses pay a steep price when we look down on the downs and outs when we should help them up. There is enormous talent strewn on our sidewalks and roadsides. I wish someone would devise a way to help avoid this situation and provide incentives for people experiencing homelessness and dropouts to become contributing citizens.

On my return drive home, I "saw" an entrepreneur, sales manager, dental hygienist, and philanthropist. What did you see on your trip home today?

Our Daughter Needed a Good Samaritan

My family visited a new church when we lived in Grand Rapids, Michigan. I could not get over how lovely the church buildings and campus were. We entered the church, looked around, and sat where we usually sit in a church: on the left side, halfway back, and on the outside aisle. The service began promptly. The sermon was excellent, and the music was good, as were the traditional hymns.

Once the worship service ended at 10:30, we planned to visit a Sunday school class. Before we could exit our seats, my daughter unexpectedly heaved, which caused some excitement. Worshipers were moving everywhere except in our direction. We are visitors and have a sick child, and we don't know where the restrooms are.

Anxiously looking around for help, we saw no one. People passed on the other side of the aisle. Everyone was continuing to their Bible study class. Finally, a lady in her 70s approached us and said, "Don't worry about the mess. The janitor will clean it up." Then she moved to the other side of the aisle.

The story of the Good Samaritan is a parable told by Jesus in the Gospel of Luke. It is about a traveler stripped of clothing, beaten, and left half dead alongside the road from Jerusalem down to Jericho. First, a priest and then a Levite come by, but both avoid the man by moving to the other side of the road.

The Bible says, "But a Samaritan came up to him on his journey, and when he saw the man, he had compassion. He went over to him and bandaged his wounds, pouring on olive oil and wine. Then he put him on his animal, took him to an inn, and cared for him. The next day, he took out two denarii, gave them to the innkeeper, and said, 'Take care of him. When I come back, I'll reimburse you for whatever extra you spend.'"

Jesus asked, "Which of these three do you think proved to be a neighbor to the man who fell into the hands of the robbers?"

"The one who showed mercy to him," he said. Then Jesus told him, "Go and do the same." (Luke 10:33–37, HCSB)

The parable is in the Bible, and the characters are real. How real are you when you come upon someone in need?

That Reminds Me of A Story

I Am God's Masterpiece

No matter the benefits of the surgery, I would rather avoid the hospital.

My wife and I sat with friends in the local hospital's pre-op room when things got tense. As directed, the friends arrived at the hospital at 6:30 a.m. for the wife to undergo a hip replacement scheduled for 9:00 a.m.

The clock on my iPhone showed 10:00 a.m., and Kathy was still in pre-op talking with us. At 10:30, the anesthesiologist explained her role in the procedure. Kathy's husband, David, interrupted her and asked if there was a problem with the operation scheduled before his wife's procedure. She explained that they were already an hour behind schedule.

The anesthesiologist's explanation was a classic in diplomacy and patient reassurance. She explained that there was no problem and that her doctor was a perfectionist. He viewed his patients as a canvas upon which he painted his flawless operation. He only finished the procedure once he had done his best work. Sometimes, it took longer than expected because of the difference in the patient's body or an unexpected obstacle. But this doctor was not to be rushed. Each operation was his masterpiece.

While we are thankful for excellent doctors who perform operations on our bodies like master artists, we are most grateful for the great artist who says, "For we are God's masterpiece. He has created us anew in Christ Jesus, so we can do the good things he planned for us long ago." (Ephesians 2:10, NLT)

I'd Get More Willies

American business executive Dee Hock once said, "The problem is never how to get new, innovative thoughts into your mind, but how to get old ones out." How do you eradicate, erase, or excise old ideas and thoughts and replace them with new views and opinions?

We all run into people with closed minds, unwilling to think or act outside the proverbial box. They fight change. Some people are for change if it doesn't affect them. Someone said there are only two types of people who like change: a cashier and a wet baby.

It's hard for a business to stay competitive when the employee's answer to change is, "We've always done it this way,"

"We've tried that before."

"You'll never get that approved."

"It costs too much."

"We've never done that."

That Reminds Me of A Story

"It isn't in the budget."

Successful change requires the support of everyone involved. The catalyst for innovation and change often comes from a team member experiencing an "aha" moment.

While conducting a Creative Off-the-Wall Thinking© workshop for a small retail company, I witnessed an aha moment that increased its sales by 19 percent at a business card cost. The retailer specializes in clothing closeouts, seconds, and odds-and-ends, and their market is primarily low-income families. Each retail store employed three to four people.

Because of a continued sales decline, the president called me and asked me to help his management team develop innovative ideas for increasing their sales. I met with his team and explained the Creative Off-the-Wall Thinking© process. We started with improving sales and identifying actions to accomplish the goal.

About 50 minutes into the session, the team had a list of ideas, including running newspaper ads, creating and mailing monthly flyers, broadcasting TV or radio commercials, conducting a sales contest among the employees, etc. The ideas were good but flawed: either they were cost-prohibitive, or the media reach didn't target their prospects.

One of my goals was to keep anyone from dominating the session and ensure that everyone contributed. I noticed that one lady had said nothing. As with any creative thinking endeavor, it is often the quiet, non-taking part of a person with a great idea. This lady felt her opinion was worthless. Maybe she had made suggestions in the past and was put down, or she sensed that someone else on the team would have the same idea if she had the idea.

As often happens in this creative environment, with ideas bouncing back and forth and people hitchhiking off each other's ideas, everyone gets excited. This session was no exception. Suddenly, without warning, the silent lady shouted, "I'd get more Willies." I wasn't sure what a "Willie" was and was hesitant to go in that direction. But I asked her to explain.

She told me she was the retail store manager and had two people working for her. On the first of each week, she received a sales report for the previous week. If sales were below average, she would go to her cashier, Willie, and say to her, "Willie, if we don't get more sales, we won't have a job!" That statement motivated Willie.

When customers came to register here to check out, Willie would suggest additional items: "Don't you want to get a shirt to match those pants or skirts?"

"That's a good price for those socks; better get another pair before they are gone."

That Reminds Me of A Story

"Did you see that half-price sales table?"

Willie practiced suggestive selling.

"So," I said, "Willie is not just a cashier; she is also a salesperson or a sales cashier."

"Yes," the manager replied.

I asked, why not give Willie a business card and print it with her new job title: Sales/Cashier? The participants were shocked. None of the retail employees had a business card.

I continued, "Why not print everyone a business card? For the shelf-stocker, make it a Sales/Inventory Replenisher. Even the employees in the home office should have cards. Buyers should be designated Sales/Buyers, truck drivers should be Sales/Drivers, and the receptionist should be Sales/Receptionist." I explained that everyone is in sales, and the closer your job is to sales, the more secure your position.

The company couldn't afford television, radio, or newspaper advertising, and these media were not assured ways to reach their target audience. However, with the small cost of business cards appropriately printed with the new job titles, the company increased its sales by 21% over the next two months.

The president said, "I wish we could get a return like that on all our investments." His investment was not in business cards; his investment improved the employees' image and importance to the company. When the individuals' self-worth goes up, sales and profits follow.

One woman, one idea, and a creative session improved sales and employee morale. Amazingly, we pay people to use their bodies and forget that their brains come along for free.

I don't suppose that this article will change the minds of big corporation CEOs or presidents. Entrepreneurs or small business owners can unlock the tremendous creative power that lies dormant in their organization. And discover more "Willies."

Why Is It Difficult to Say "Thank You?"

I go to the same donut shop twice a week, and each morning, I order the same thing: coffee, black, and a cinnamon roll, nothing else, never anything different. When I enter the shop, any of the four employees—who automatically pour my coffee and never ask if I want sugar or cream—go to the display case and choose a cinnamon roll. Then, they come to the counter and say, "Two dollars." Over 100 times, I have repeated this ritual, and only once has any employee stated, "Thank You."

I have witnessed how difficult it is for some people to say, "Thank

That Reminds Me of A Story

You." But, saying thank you for a business transaction, opening the door for someone, or even helping a little old lady across the street pales compared to stating thank you to people who have influenced our lives. The actions, advice, and lifestyle of family, friends, neighbors, teachers, coaches, pastors, priests, rabbis, and business associates influence our lives and help determine our journey.

Ann Landers, an advice columnist writer, asked, "Why is it so difficult to thank people who have influenced our lives?" Ann wisely wrote that there are two primary reasons we cannot say thank you. First, people intend to do it, but many find it hard to put their feelings into words. The second reason is our nature to procrastinate. We mean well but never get around to it until it is often too late.

Those two excuses for not saying thank you struck a chord with me. I determined I would not be guilty of failing to thank the extraordinary people who had a significant role in making me who I am.

Some people believed in you when you didn't believe in yourself, encouraged you when you were uninspired, provided direction when you were lost, and stood by you when you felt alone. These people recall the words of Guillaume Apollinaire, "Come to the edge," he said.

They said, "We are afraid. Come to the edge," he stated. They came. He pushed them, and they flew."

We need to invite others to the edge and push them into flight.

The Master of Truth

The early morning knock on the door startled and awoke the Master, Chen Ka Ming.

"Who is there?" he said.

"It is me, your disciple, Cho Lo."

Shaking the morning fog from his head, the Master invited Cho to enter and tell him what he wanted. Cho entered the room, bowed reverently, and spoke quietly, "Master, I wish to know the truth."

"Young disciple," the Master said, "You are not alone in the quest for truth. All my disciples come to me and seek the answer to the same question. The answer is always the same; the truth is the love that bonds society." Truth is reality. We do not create truth, design, or manufacture it; we discover it. To know the truth, one must find it.

Then the ancient Master said, "Cho Lo, I taught you that there is no truth from childhood onward. People grow up with this idea and learn that every thought, belief, and principle is flexible. Facts are scalable and present the views of the speaker."

One day, after you have grown accustomed to opening your mind to new thoughts, you'll understand that the Great Master doesn't describe truth as the opposite of falsity. He took falsity and, out of it, created the truth: He is love.

The Master's Five Precepts

- Truth is not seen nor heard; we experience it.
- Never get so fascinated with the fact that you cannot check its authenticity. It is valid only if verifiable.
- The night cannot darken the truth. Truth is light, but light is not the truth.
- Truth isn't in a golden crown but a crown of thorns.
- Refrain from being the author of truth.

Cho Lo knelt and, without hesitation, said. "Master, now I understand. You have helped me see that the truth is love."

There Are Well-Mannered People

There are well-mannered people and bad-mannered people in the world. The same opportunities are presented to the same people all their lives because they show either manners or lack of manners. There is no in-between.

Holding the door for a lady or senior couple to enter a building exemplifies politeness. A well-mannered person says, "Here, let me get that door."

"Thank you for holding the door." The bad-mannered person jumps ahead of a lady with a cane and acts as if no one is standing there.

In a restaurant, a well-mannered patron thanks the cashier for taking their order. A bad-mannered cashier puts the change in the patron's hand and moves on to the next customer.

Driving in traffic separates the well-mannered from the bad-mannered. The good-mannered people slow when the light turns yellow. The bad-mannered people close their eyes and barrel through the red light.

Well-mannered people drive through the neighborhood slowly, watching for kids. Poor-mannered people race through the area like they are targeting kids. Well-mannered people RSVP an invitation. Those with bad manners don't remember to accept the invitation yet still show up.

I will not tell you which kind I am but don't attend my party without making a reservation.

That Reminds Me of A Story

When You Know Little

It's nice that we have so many outlets to shop for phones and that the retailers provide customer service and information when required. In my experience, most sales/service employees are knowledgeable and friendly.

Today, I took my iPhone to a local AT&T phone service store. When a customer service rep asked to describe my problem, I said, "My phone doesn't ring when I receive a call. My wife's phone does."

I glanced around the store; I saw six other customers and three more waiting for help. All the customers looked over seventy and had puzzled faces. I knew I fit right in. I'm 81.

After entering my password, I handed my phone to my sales/service representative (pretty good for an older man to know that trick). He solved my problem immediately. There are two buttons on the top left side of the phone. As he explained, the top one increases volume, and the bottom one decreases volume. The rep pushed the top button about six times and handed the phone back to me. Then, he asked for my phone number, and I gave it to him. He took out his phone and dialed the numbers I provided. I knew he had dialed the number I passed him because, to my chagrin, my cell phone was loudly ringing. Magic, no. The rep knew what to do: push the top left-side button six times.

I hope the other nine older customers know about the two buttons on their phone's top left-hand side.

Fingerprints, Snowflakes, and You

You will never build a strong, positive relationship with anyone else—until you have a solid, positive, accepting relationship with yourself.

Here are four guidelines to follow in creating a better self-image.

Accept yourself. Accepting yourself begins with the thought that you are unique, unlike any other person. Like fingerprints and snowflakes, you are amazing. However, you are important; never confuse the idea of importance with self-importance.

If you accept yourself, you must get past the idea that some people are more important than others. Often, we prioritize or judge people, including ourselves, according to a counterfeit status code. The guidelines may be wealth, power, education, physical appearance, nationality, occupation, or other outward class signs. Accept yourself.

Appreciate yourself, which is another way of saying you have healthy self-esteem and feel good about yourself.

People appreciate themselves in direct proportion to their self-esteem. Esteem means to value. Therefore, self-esteem is how much you love yourself. I experience that others will respect you no more than you respect yourself. Someone wisely stated, "If you put a small value on yourself, rest assured that the world will not raise your price."

My parents taught me that there is nothing more important in relationship building than the value you put on yourself. "You see in others," my father would say, "what you see in yourself." If you like yourself, you will like others. If you dislike yourself, you will have a dislike for others.

Your potential reflects your strengths and weaknesses. But it's your strengths that can truly propel you forward. Building strong relationships, achieving success all hinges on identifying and using your unique talents. As Marcus Buckingham and Donald O. Clifton wrote, "Unfortunately, most of us have little sense of our talents and strengths, much less the ability to build lives around them. Instead, guided by our parents, teachers, managers, and psychology's fascination with pathology, we become experts in our weaknesses and spend our lives trying to repair flaws. At the same time, our strengths lie dormant and neglected."

Discover your strengths and then play to these strengths.

Acknowledge success, which is achieving what you want to attain unencumbered by the judgment of others. We must acknowledge success because everyone has experienced success in some form, some more than others. Often, people will downplay their achievements or credit them to luck because of a lack of self-esteem. The size of success doesn't matter. As someone has described, luck is what you have left over after giving 100 percent.

It does not matter how you slice or dice it. Success is a success. We best acknowledge our success when we use it as a foundation to build on for our subsequent success. And we must never forget that success, like failure, is repeatable.

Accept yourself for who you are. Be comfortable with yourself, but never complacent. Everyone has room for growth.

A Servant Leader is the Phantom that Empowers Others

If there has ever been a book written about being a lousy leader and getting people not to follow you, I've never seen it. Today, everything is about leading and leadership.

I don't know whether it's me or the times, but defining "leadership" and "servant leadership" is easy. A leader leads: while blending into the background, a servant leader serves his followers by providing the support, direction, encouragement, and discipline they need to achieve their goals. The servant leader, like a supporting actor, makes stars of others.

That Reminds Me of A Story

One exciting aspect of leadership is that it's often situational. Sometimes, we lead, and usually, we follow. In either case, we are called to discharge our duties in the service of others. Before we serve, we learn to serve.

In business, there's a hierarchy of employment roles: worker, supervisor/manager, boss, leader, and servant-leader. Few are at the servant-leader pinnacle, and lucky are the people serving beside the servant-leader.

Lao Tzu, the ancient Chinese philosopher and poet, described a leader this way. "A leader is best when people barely know he exists. When his work is done and his aim is fulfilled, they will say: We did it ourselves."

So, when you hear a leader respond, "Yes, you did."

You are with a servant leader.

The Not-So-Secret Sabotage

A couple of friends tell this story. They arrived for the closing of a building they owned. They were to meet an employee of the closing firm, whom they had spoken to several times over the phone. She had given them the time and date of the closing.

The couple arrived at 8:30 A.M. as instructed. They discovered no one at the receptionist's desk entering the office. After several callouts, "Hello, anyone home?" a woman came out of the back and asked them (curtly), "What do you want?"

The couple introduced themselves and waited for the woman to say her name or, at least, to shake hands. Neither action happened. Pamela said, "We are here as instructed by your company to complete the closure of our building."

The woman answered, "O yeah, you're buying a building."

"No," the lady said, "we are selling our building."

"We've been dealing with Jane. Is she in?"

"Yeah, but she is too busy checking her emails to come out for the signing. I'll handle this. No worry." Then she disappeared. After eight minutes, the employee returned with the paperwork.

She ushered the couple into a room to sign the papers. Because the lady had not introduced herself, the seller finally offered her hand to the woman. The woman replied, "Yes, I made a copy of your ID."

After handing the documents to the couple, she instructed them to sign, "Here, here, here, and here." They signed four times. The woman said nothing, took the forms, and disappeared down the hall.

Ten minutes went by, and no one came out. The couple got up and started toward the door when they noticed a plaque on the wall. It

That Reminds Me of A Story

read, "2017 Real Estate Title Closing Center of The Year."

One Well-Told Story Packs More Power Than 1,000 Business Cards

"If history were taught in the form of stories, it would never be forgotten." —Rudyard Kipling.

Stories have the power to engage people at a whole new level.

A good story is simple to remember because it is a picture painted with words. For example, take the classic tale of the three little pigs who built their houses from different materials. The first pig made his house of straw, the second pig fashioned his house using sticks, and the third pig used bricks to construct a wonderful home.

The house constructed of bricks was sturdy and resisted the huffing and puffing of the big bad wolf. When confronted by the wolf, the other two little pigs escape their easily destroyed houses and find safety in the third little pig's house of bricks.

When the two pigs, with destroyed houses, rebuilt, they built with bricks. It was hard work, but when they were completed, the other two little pigs felt safe and lived happily ever after.

I know you didn't ask, but here are some thoughts on creating a great story. I don't have all the guidelines, but the first rule is that great storytelling begins with a great story. Pass out your business card if you don't have something worth saying.

A good story should have these elements to engage an audience.

Attention. Immediately grab your audience's attention and invite the audience to listen further.

Present one idea. Using familiar words, sounds, and images to communicate an identifiable message. One story. One focus. The goal is to make a point, not points.

Resonate with your audience. Good stories engage people's emotions. If the story is believable, people quickly connect with you and the story.

Invite people to respond. The best stories are positive and uplifting and offer a better life for people.

Lasting. Like an excellent wine, good stories are memorable and improve over time. Listeners retell your story to others, expanding the story's outreach and broadening your influence.

Good storytelling is an art.

Put Your Opinions to the Test

Have you ever thought your opinions may not resonate with others?

That Reminds Me of A Story

The next time you speak, don't listen to yourself talking. Observe the reactions of others to what you say. Or ask them to repeat what you stated. What you see and what you hear may surprise you.

Occasionally, you'll encounter people who refuse to take a stance on a subject. This indifferent stance may be helpful when they want to be unbiased or have no particular interest in it.

Be prepared when you ask someone for their opinion. For example, "What's your opinion on American politics?" Usually, you'll get a diverse and robust range of views.

Do your opinions pass the validity test? To confirm your views, ask yourself these questions:

- Is my opinion based on facts?
- Is my opinion based on firsthand experience or secondary information?
- Is my opinion biased?
- Am I open to the views of others?

When we voice our opinions, we state our worldview — how we see things. The people you know and the places that shape your beliefs. Others may not be acquainted with all the people you know; they haven't experienced the same places, or associated with the same people, and don't share the same education. There is no one like you.

There is wisdom in caution: "Be careful with a view or judgment formed about something not based on fact or knowledge."

Setting New Year's Resolutions

Every action has two outcomes: success or failure. It's that simple. People prefer success. I don't think I have met anyone whose goal is to fail, but failure happens. Our response to failure determines whether we become successful.

When successful people fail, they learn from the experience and then move on—the wiser—to try again. They don't see failure as a final but as a learning experience. Here are ten ideas for obtaining success in the New Year.

- Determine where you want to be next year. Knowing the goal enables you to work backward, setting small, specific, and well-planned actions to achieve the goal. Learn why—the exact purpose—you want to accomplish and move toward it with each action step.

- Establish accountability. Say, "I got this one." Accept responsibility and accountability for your actions.

- Expect and prepare for the unexpected. Peter's Law states, "The unexpected always happens." Before finalizing your new year's goals, conduct a "What if" exercise. If this happens, I will do this.

- Develop a can-do attitude. Success requires an inner drive and a positive attitude.

- Have an innovative spirit. Always look for ways to innovate and improve every activity you engage in.

- Keep your knowledge current and your skills marketable. The person who improves their knowledge and occupation skills will be ready when an opportunity arises.

- Be a problem solver. Evaluate the facts to discover the solution hidden within the problem. Identify the solution hidden within the issue.

- Never lose sight of the goal. Engage in activities that advance you to your destination and avoid activities that detract from it.

- Focus on results, not on being busy. Never confuse activity with results. Spend time on the activities that matter most to you.

- Celebrate and have fun. Balance a strong work ethic with a timely victory celebration. Your goal should be to celebrate the results, not the activities.

Guard Against Idea Assassins

Finding solutions to problems always involves high uncertainty. In the search for innovative ideas, you're sailing upon uncharted waters. Your creative team may fear the unknown, like the ancient mariners who feared sea serpents.

Often, you will not know where you're going until you get there in creative problem-solving. As you sail forward, you make discoveries that add to your knowledge about the problem and come closer to discovering the solution you seek.

Two travelers were talking one day about their travel plans. The first traveler questioned the second traveler about why he preferred to take a train over an airplane. "Is it because of your fear of flying?" he asked.

"No," replied the second traveler.

"It's my fear of crashing."

Nothing is more fatal to creativity than the fear of failure. Many individuals aren't afraid of creative thinking; they are worried their ideas will be laughed at and ridiculed. So, like the non-flyer, they don't venture forth. They aren't willing to expose themselves to the chance of "crashing."

Idea production involves taking risks. Those risks include being laughed at or ridiculed, looking foolish, and losing self-esteem. The pressure created by fear can impede a person's creative abilities.

It is crucial to shift from a negative mindset, which can stifle ideas before they even take shape, to a more positive one that encourages and nurtures creativity within your organization. This shift can significantly boost morale and productivity.

Here are a few examples of Idea Assassin's killer statements:

- Don't be ridiculous.
- We've never done it before.
- We've tried that before.
- It isn't in the budget.
- It won't work in our industry.
- If it were a good idea, someone else would do it.
- That's not the business we are in.

Encourage people to challenge assumptions and question the way things are done. Eliminate obstacles that prevent team members from making suggestions.

Wayne Nalls

Aging

"Getting old is like climbing a mountain; you get a little out of breath, but the view is much better!" - Ingrid Bergman.

Aging is a force that can either control us or be controlled by us; it's a matter of perspective. Wrinkles, a waning desire for activity, memory loss, and feelings of frustration and anger can all be part of the aging process. While we often notice these signs in others, we may overlook the fact that we, too, are aging.

While viewing the internet today, I witnessed growing old. On the internet was a posting of stars and comparing pictures of famous people from the 50s, 60s, and 70s. Even the "beautiful" people age; some are unrecognizable in their senior years. The comparable pictures of Donnie Osmond, Ann Margret, Annette Funicello, Sally Field, and Paul Anka reveal the external signs of the aging story.

Aging is normal and affects everyone biologically, psychologically, and socially. Natural aging happens, but a healthy lifestyle may help you live longer. Certain drugs, strong relationships, reading, and puzzle-solving may help with psychological aging. Staying positive can increase longevity and aid recovery from disability.

Learn to live your best life and maintain physical, psychological, social, and mental health. Accept your age. Aging is inevitable, and embracing it can make all the difference.

That Reminds Me of A Story

When I compare my younger pictures with my photos of today, even though I am not a star, I have, like Paul Anka, aged.

Where did the U.S.A. Today Go?

When I opened the door to my hotel room this morning, I noticed something funny. When I looked down at the doorway, I did not see the U.S.A. Today newspaper.

Thinking someone had forgotten to place the paper there, I went to the receptionist's desk and asked for a copy. The clerk's response to my request was unforgettable. She asked, "What is a U.S.A. today?" I responded and told her it was a newspaper. Her next question helped explain America's plight — "What is a newspaper?"

Her question also shows that I haven't recently stayed in Hampton Inn.

People Are Different

To build strong relationships with others, we must know our character and then seek to understand others' character. It is important because only by learning one's character can one relate to others and avoid misunderstandings.

We deal with four distinct types of people daily. I am using the members of a football team as an example.

The Quarterback — Task-oriented and impulsive, they have high expectations. Appear confident, persuasive, verbal, aggressive, and autocratic. Quarterbacks are in charge and call the plays. These play-callers are very punctual and demand the same from others. They are not overly social-minded. They initiate the call to go to lunch.

The Running Back—These people are enthusiastic, inspirational, and imaginative. They like working with visuals, ideas, and words. They are curious and independent. When dealing with these individuals, avoid too much detail. When invited to lunch, they don't care where they eat.

The Blocker — Characterized as a team player, friendly, eager to help, and relationship-oriented. They identify with goals and activities approved by others. It may take some time to get to know these people. Once you do, you have a powerful ally in your relationship with others. Invited to lunch, they don't care where they are dining if the team eats together.

The Referee — These individuals strongly identify with rules and regulations; the best way is the organization. They are fond of saying, "That's how we do things around here; it's the NFL policy." They are conservative but unimaginative, preferring technical calls. When asked about lunch, they ask, "Who is paying?"

That Reminds Me of A Story

Being sensitive to this uniqueness in yourself and others will help you. How people act is who they are.

OCD

People who say, "I would like to know that person better," "I wish I understood my coworkers," or "I would be more confident if I were a member of that group" have the motivation to build stronger relationships.

Last night, my wife and I enjoyed two episodes of Mr. Monk on Amazon Prime. I don't know how I missed viewing the original 125 episodes. The show's star, Adrian Monk, is an ex-prominent homicide detective in the San Francisco Police Department who has a pervasive preoccupation with orderliness, perfectionism, and control (OCD) but continues to solve crimes.

In the movie As Good as It Gets, the lead character, Jack Nicholson's Melvin, is at war with his world, tyrannizing his neighbors and all who cross his carefully ordered path. But he meets a server, Carol (Helen Hunt), at his local diner, who changes his life. At one point, the changed Melvin tells Carol, "You make me a better man."

The person with OCD has uncontrollable, reoccurring thoughts and behaviors that they feel the urge to repeat repeatedly. Many people who don't have OCD still exhibit habits they repeat over and over. Past failures become a mantra, reminding us that we will never be happy and prosperous.

Don't avoid the cracks in the sidewalk of life. Don't let unreasonable thoughts and fears (obsessions) lead you to compulsive behaviors. You can change. Turn your persistent preoccupation with orderliness, perfectionism, fears, and anxieties to God. He will make you a better person.

SECTION 10:
GROWING UP

Stories as seen through the lens of maturing.

I Still Have Dreams

Two senior women were talking in the waiting room of a doctor's office. Both reminded me of Susan Boyle of Britain's Got Talent, a little overweight, frumpy, disheveled gray hair, and I was soon to witness another trait, wisdom, where wisdom was unexpected.

I overheard one lady complaining about the waiting time, her physical aches and pains, and her medicine price. She handed the other lady a piece of paper and asked her to read it; the type was too small.

The second lady only commented that I couldn't see anything but still had dreams. She couldn't see but thought of the future.

The first woman was miserable and wanted her friend to commiserate with her. In the second lady's comment, I heard Susan Boyle singing the second verse of "Les Misérables."

I dreamed a dream in times gone by

When hope was high and life worth living

I dreamed that love would never die

I dreamed that God would be forgiving

Then, I was young and unafraid

And dreams were made and used and wasted

That Reminds Me of A Story

There was no ransom to be paid

Yes, the second lady has a dream, but days haven't passed. She is still dreaming. Victor Hugo, the writer of Les Misérables, says, "There is nothing like a dream to create the future."

Here is a small snippet from the song's first verse.

And the World was a song

And the song was exciting

There was a time

The second lady knows her remaining time is short, and she plans on filling the days with endless wonder. She dreams.

Looking Back

Looking back on a beautiful memory is one of the pleasures of life, and this story is about one such memorable time.

I remember the neighborhood I grew up in. Five wooden houses were on each side of the road; each had two bedrooms and one bath. Unfortunately, there were no attached garages. Several had a front porch with a swing, including ours. We did not have carpet or tile, only wood floors, except in the kitchen, we had linoleum.

We had electricity and running water, but my parents got our first house phone (dial-up) in 1947; I was seven years old. Our number was 629-1715, with no area code. We were on a "party line," meaning others could pick up their phone and listen to the conversation.

The driveways were dirt, excellent for shooting marbles and looking for doodlebugs. To see a doodlebug, you placed a finger in its hole and sang, "Doodlebug, doodlebug, come out. Your house is on fire." Yards were grass you mowed with a rotary push mower, but there were no power mowers.

Stinging nettles were everywhere, and we knew their sting well from running barefooted through the woods behind our house. I don't know if that plant is still around or has become extinct. No one has mentioned a stinging nettle in the last forty years, but you remember the sharp pain if it stung you.

In the 40s, our neighbors knew us, and we knew them. Any neighborhood parent could discipline you if they catch you doing something wrong. My brother and I agreed. We preferred the neighbor's discipline rather than reporting our actions to our parents, who disciplined us.

Freedom best describes my neighborhood. We were free to play any game we wanted, be open to associating with all the neighborhood kids, and engage in a discussion. We then moved on to the next activity, free to expand to include the three streets south and the four

That Reminds Me of A Story

streets west.

I remember well the neighborhood fish fry. Several dads fished all day, brought their catch home, cleaned them, and deep-fried them in a big black kettle filled with hot grease (from the wood fire beneath it). When the fish was done, someone would spoon the dough for the hushpuppies. The mothers brought fresh vegetables, pickles, homemade desserts, and tea.

After saying grace, we ate.

I still remember the wood fire, boiling grease, onions in the hushpuppies, and the taste of fresh, deep-fried fish from 75 years ago.

As much as I loved that neighborhood, there's a downside to it. My children and grandchildren will never experience dirt driveways, linoleum floors, dial phones, shooting marbles, or running barefoot through the stinging nettles. The problem is that today's children will not experience a neighborhood fish fry with hushpuppies, pecan pie, and neighbors who love them.

Learning to Drive

One of life's keystones is getting your driver's license. When you turn sixteen, you can obtain a permit to drive. Most of the kids I knew got their licenses soon after their 16th birthday.

I wasn't an exception.

My mother went with me to get a driver's license handbook. I soon learned the signs — stop, slow down, right and left turn, school zone, etc. Again, my mother drove me to the highway patrol station to take the test. Before testing me, the officer asked me to read the letters on the room's eye chart. To my surprise, I couldn't read any of them. The test ended there, and my mother scheduled an appointment with an optometrist.

The optometrist determined I needed glasses. No, I thought, cool guys, don't wear glasses. A newly visible world opened when I returned to the optometrist's office and fitted my glasses. I could see what I had missed. I soon discovered I could read the books' titles on the bookstore's bottom shelves without bending down.

I returned to the exam center at the highway patrol center and passed the written part of my test. Now, it was time to learn to drive. During this time, I realized my mother had patience and wisdom.

Learning to drive a stick-shift car wasn't easy. Mother preserved. She told me hundreds of times, "Slow down." She provided the three best pieces of driving advice: 1. If you're in an accident, don't leave the scene. 2. Always pull over and stop when a police officer signals you to do so. 3. As you drive, keep the center of the front hood aligned with the road's edge, and you know you're in your driving lane.

That Reminds Me of A Story

Once I saw and applied my mother's advice, I passed the driver's test and got my learner's permit. I never enjoyed wearing eyeglasses.

Growing Up

I remember the neighborhood I grew up in. Five wooden houses were on each side of the road, each with two bedrooms and one bath. Unfortunately, there were no attached garages. Several houses, including ours, had a front porch with a swing. We did not have carpet or tile, only wood floors. The exception was in the kitchen; we had linoleum.

The driveways were dirt, excellent for shooting marbles and looking for doodlebugs. To see a doodlebug, you placed a finger in its hole and sang, "Doddle bug, doddle bug, come out; your house is on fire." Yards were grass you mowed with a rotary push mower. but There were no power mowers.

Stinging nettles were everywhere, and we knew their sting well from running barefooted through the woods behind our house. I don't know if that plant is still around or has become extinct. No one has mentioned a stinging nettle in the last forty years, but you remember the sharp pain if it stung you.

In the 40s, our neighbors knew us, and we knew them. Any

neighborhood parent could discipline you if they catch you doing something wrong. My brother and I agree; we preferred the neighbor's discipline rather than them reporting our actions to our parents and then. They discipline us.

Freedom best describes my neighborhood. We were free to play any game, open to associating with all the neighborhood kids, engage in a heated discussion, and then move on to the next activity. We could expand our area to include the three streets south and the four streets west.

I remember well the neighborhood fish fry. Several dads fished all day. They brought their catch home, cleaned them, and deep-fried them in a big black kettle filled with hot grease (from the wood fire beneath it). When the fish was done, someone would spoon in the dough for the hushpuppies. The mothers brought fresh vegetables, pickles, homemade desserts, and tea. After the blessing, we ate.

I still remember the wood fire, the boiling grease, the onions, and the savory taste of the fish. As much as I loved that neighborhood, it has a downside.

My grandchildren won't experience dirt driveways, linoleum floors, dial phones, shooting marbles, or running barefoot through the stinging nettles. The problem is that today's children will not experience a neighborhood fish fry with hushpuppies, pecan pies, and neighbors who love them.

That Reminds Me of A Story

Lessons Learned Early Are Better Than Lessons Learned Late

Here are five of my favorite business lessons from my early teenage years. Quickly learned lessons from mowing lawns and delivering newspapers still serve as success guidelines.

As a youngster, I was ambitious. My first job was cutting my neighbor's grass. As I recall, I earned fifty cents per hour while mowing lawns. And the money was all mine. My dad provided the mower and gas.

I soon added a paper route to my budding entrepreneurial endeavor. I sold a door-to-door weekly paper—The Marion Sun — for ten cents and got a nickel for each newspaper I sold. I quickly became the number one sales boy and received a weekly silver dollar from the publisher for this achievement.

I wasn't afraid of hard work. I willingly went door-to-door, asking people if I could mow their yards. I also questioned if they wanted to buy a newspaper with the latest local news. I knew nothing about business planning, goals, strategy, or tactics at this stage. I only knew I had to ask for the order to make a sale. So, I requested the opportunity. I learned that not everyone had to say "Yes" people to keep me busy.

By my fourteenth birthday, I was a capitalist, entrepreneur, and small business owner by my fourteenth birthday. I learned responsibility and the connection between effort and reward. Here are five lessons I learned as a teenager that may prove valuable to you on your successful journey.

If I worked, I would get paid. Success is about getting the proper results. When I mowed the yard or delivered the paper, they paid me. If I failed to work, I would receive nothing.

Self-discipline is essential in setting priorities. There are many activities a youngster can engage in. My parents' help taught me that school was priority number one because it brought immediate payoff and a much more critical long-term success. So, I arranged after-school and weekend work time around school attendance and homework. I chose long-term success over short-term enjoyment—radio, games, and comic books.

The customer defines customer service. Customers determined whether I had done an excellent job mowing their lawns or delivering their papers. It wasn't how hard I worked or how long it took that decided their satisfaction. The customer's perception of the yard's appearance or that the paper was on time determined satisfaction.

Responsibility comes with the job. Unfortunately, many people do not want to accept responsibility. These risk-avoiders believe the less obligation they have, the safer their position. The more accountable you are, the more secure your job. People willing to take responsibility are rare.

Have the proper tools for the job. Like many jobs, the work is more comfortable with the right tools. My tools were a lawnmower, a bicycle, and a passion for success. The business world requires tools other than a lawnmower and a bike. But all jobs have one primary tool: a shared love. A person with a passion for excellence and the proper tools is always in demand.

Battle Creek, Michigan

What is the first city name you remember besides your hometown? My hometown is Ocala, FL, and Battle Creek, Michigan, is the first city I knew outside my town. Why Battle Creek? It is the birthplace of the cereal industry.

For over 100 years, Cereal City has been the hub of breakfast cereal production in the United States. In a study, the authors concluded that Cap'n Crunch would remain the crispest in milk for the most extended time without becoming completely soggy. Consumers overwhelmingly favor Frosted Flakes as Kellogg's best-selling cereal.

As a kid, I liked Raisin Brand, Wheaties, Merita Bread, and Ovaltine. What I craved was the box tops and labels on the products. You sent those items to Battle Creek to receive free prizes: A Long

Ranger mask and a silver bullet pencil sharpener, a Tom Mix decoder ring, and a Sky King compass, among other child-thrilling items.

I remember getting the box tops, placing them in an envelope, and sending them to Battle Creek. There were no zip codes. The Post Office Department introduced the Zone Improvement Plan (ZIP) Code in 1963.

Merita Bread or Wheaties and the Battle Creek, Michigan, address brought the prize. You mailed your letter one day and expected to receive your prize the next day. But delivery didn't happen the next day, and no FedEx existed.

Maybe the delay—about two weeks—provided your anticipation-excitement for fourteen days.

The Broken Twig on Mother's Azalea Bush

Someone said mothers have eyes on the back of their heads. This expression is typically used to convey a mother's intuitive knowledge. It is an idiom that says someone has seen or noticed something wrong.

My mother had eyes on the back of her head.

One day, my brother and I were throwing a football in our front yard.

That Reminds Me of A Story

As young kids will do, we got rowdy and careless and accidentally tossed the ball into Mother's azalea bush, breaking a small twig off near the bottom of the plant. Instantly, we knew we were in trouble. We quickly devised a plan to mix mud and attempt to glue the twig back onto the bush where it was initially.

Eureka, it worked, and we returned to throwing the football.

Later, when Mother came out to check what we were doing, she immediately recognized something was wrong with her brush. The broken twig was still on the bush where it originally was. Yet she sensed something was out of place and said, "Who broke the limb off my bush?"

Only two boys were standing in the yard, and one had a football in his hand. Both knew they were in trouble. Mother knew.

We broke the twig on your. She said because I have eyes on the back of my head! My brother and I looked; we did not see the eyes she spoke of. But we acknowledged she could see the broken twig we had tried to reattach. We also recognize that we faced punishment, not for breaking the bush, but for attempting to cover it up.

Thomas and His New Glove

Thomas was not shy about his new first baseman's glove. It was new and big. The rest of our team used old gloves purchased at a local pawnshop or yard sale. Our gloves were smaller but did the same as Tomas' mitt, protecting the hand while catching a baseball.

There was a time in baseball history when the players preferred to catch the ball with their bare hands lest they be called a "sissy" or a "softy" for wearing a glove. 12-year-old Thomas was not a sissy. He was 5' 6" tall and weighed 155 pounds.

When we went out on the field, Thomas took his position at first base, clutching his new glove. I was the center fielder. Our shirts didn't have numbers or names, but team members knew I was #7: The New York Yankees, Mickey Mantle.

After the umpire said, "Play ball," we took to the field.

The first two innings were scoreless. Because we were the home team, our opponents batted first in the third. Their leadoff batter swung on the first pitch and popped a high foul ball toward first base, where Tomas was.

Thomas positioned himself under the ball and raised his glove to catch it. But in doing so, he blocked his view of the ball. Now, every baseball player knows they must keep their eyes on the ball. Our first baseman shifted his bigger-than-life glove to find the ball. He didn't see the ball; the ball found him. When Thomas moved his glove in a split second, the ball hit him on his head.

That Reminds Me of A Story

Keeping your eye on the ball is a way of reminding people to pay attention to a situation. Stay focused on their task or goal, even when they can't see the ball.

Today, concentrate on achieving your specific achievable goals. Keep your eye on the ball and get precisely what you want.

Killing Without Motive Is Still Murder

Being only eleven years old and a boy, my idea of crime was listening to "Crime Busters" on the radio, reading about the stories of Dick Tracy in the newspaper, or allowing my mind to engage in a crime comic. The crime was big in Gotham City, but Batman controlled it.

On April 13, 1951, the killing of a sheriff in my hometown, Ocala, Florida, put a face on crime. That day, Marion County Sheriff Edward Porter Jr. was found savagely stabbed with an ice pick six times and shot to death in his wrecked car on an isolated road four miles west of Ocala.

Within two days, a suspect, a 16-year-old, confessed to the murder. Motive is often challenging to determine, but not in this case. When the state attorney asked his motive, the youth said, "I had none."

Our attitude about events has the power to transition and transform our lives. Many events are expected, and others suddenly appear without warning. A day can bring joy or devastation, flowers or rain. Excellent motivation produces excellence, while lacking motivation can lead to disaster.

This wasn't a Crime Stopper or Dick Tracy's made-up crime story. It was an actual murder that happened in my hometown. (1951 population of 38,000).

Today, Ocala is home to over 400 thoroughbred farms and training centers and has a population of 63,591. Most citizens are unaware of this event that happened seventy-three years ago.

First Date

There was this young girl who invited me to go to a movie. I accepted the invitation. Before her brother, his date, and his sister arrived to pick me up, my mother reminded me that I was to pay for my date's movie ticket. So, I put an extra fifty cents in my pocket.

We drove to the theater, enjoyed the movie, and headed home. When we arrived at her home, her brother stopped the car, and we all sat there. It was uncomfortable, and finally, my date opened her door and ran to the front porch.

I am sure she remembers this date. I do. This wasn't her first date, but it was mine. I did not buy her popcorn or a drink and missed the opportunity to walk her to her door. Later, I learned that saying "good night" could be the highlight of a date.

Two Job Applicants and One Job

When I was fifteen, my friend and I applied for a summer job at a local grocery store. The store manager talked with us and liked both of us. He said one of us could have the grocery-bagging job.

I looked at my friend and knew I would lose him if I chose the job. He glanced at me and realized he might lose my friendship if he took the job. Neither of us claimed the job. We decided friendship was more important than bagging groceries. We also learned never to apply for a job together.

Wayne Nalls

SECTION 11:
STORIES I HAVE READ WHILE SITTING ON MY FRONT PORCH

Stories are seen through maturing.

That Reminds Me of A Story

Awareness is a Powerful Word

A line in the song "Do You Believe In Magic" goes, "The magic is in the music, and the music is in me." For many people, that's where their music remains.

Dr. Randy Pausch was not such a man. He died at age 47, before his time. Pausch, a computer science professor and virtual reality pioneer, died of complications from pancreatic cancer. His fame resulted from his "Last Lecture." This lecture was part of a long-standing academic tradition at Carnegie Mellon. Pausch agreed to give the speech. A month before delivering it, Pausch's doctor told him he was in the terminal disease's early stages.

The book, "The Last Lecture," based on Pausch's last lecture, became a No. 1 bestseller with over five million copies sold.

On achieving dreams, Dr. Pausch said, "It's not about achieving your dreams; it's about how to live your life." He continued, "Life is not complicated and unfair." The ancient Greek philosopher Epictetus said, "See things for what they are. Things and people are not what we wish them to be or what they seem to be. They are what they are. When something happens, the only thing within your power is your attitude toward it; you can either accept it or resent it."

Pausch uses an example of brick walls as his focus: "The brick is not there to keep us out. The brick walls are there to give us a chance to show how badly we want something. Because the brick walls are there to stop the people who don't want it badly enough, they're there to stop the OTHER people."

Brick walls, roadblocks, obstacles- however you describe adversity standing between you and brick walls and enjoy the challenge of moving around, under, or through them. Seek the goal on the other side of the wall, and nothing can keep me from achieving your dream.

Readers Like Fishermen, Don't Let the Big Ones Get Away

I read books for pleasure, information, and application. Two books I recently read meet this criterion.

One of the non-fiction books deals with the 2006 disastrous climb of Mt. Everest. This other book is a work of fiction about a shepherd boy's quest to find a treasure in the Pyramids of Egypt, only to discover it back home. I classify both books, Into Thin Air and The Alchemist, as "fishing" books. I am not talking about outdoor, deep-sea, or ice fishing. I refer to these books as having a fishing hook that catches the reader.

Read a few pages of either book, and you're hooked. On the recommendation of two friends, I purchased the books. Without their suggestions, I may have missed being blessed by Jon Krakauer, author of Into Thin Air, and Paulo Coelho, author of The Alchemist. People read books for many reasons. But the content of a book should make us better people and, therefore, more successful.

The Alchemist provides two excellent examples of ideas with the power to increase our chances of success. In the book, a camel driver tells the shepherd boy why he's not concerned with the threat of war surrounding them: "Because I don't live in either my past or my future. I'm interested only in the present. You'll be fortunate if you can always concentrate on the present."

Later, the shepherd boy explained what alchemists do. "They show that when we strive to become better than we are, everything around us becomes better, too." The better salesperson has better customers and works for the better company. A better doctor heals more people and saves more lives. The better the entertainer provides excellent entertainment: the better the teacher, the better the students. And the better neighbor lives in a better neighborhood.

A Person is A Person, No Matter How Small

In Dr. Seuss' book, "Horton Hears a Who," Horton, an elephant, is the only one who hears an entire tiny city of people (Whoville) inside a speck of dust on a flower.

Horton stands up for the speck, saying, "Everyone deserves respect." Horton is a bridge between the Whos and the Jungle of Nool. By taking a positive stance, Horton promotes a lesson of speaking out and being involved—one we should learn.

The Old Testament tells the story of a young Israelite enslaved girl serving in the house of a Syrian general named Naaman. The young girl was captured in a raid and taken back to Syria to help General Naaman's wife. She liked Naaman and his wife. But Naaman was a leper.

The young servant girl, a "Horton" with no credentials, said to her mistress, "If only my master went to the prophet who is in Samaria, he would cure him of his skin disease." So Naaman told his master what the girl from the land of Israel had said. Therefore, the king of Aram said, "Go, and I will send a letter with you to the king of Israel." (2 Kings 5:4, 5, HCSB)

When Elisha heard Naaman's appearance distressed the king before him, he sent the king a message, "Why have you torn your clothes? Have him come to me; he will know a prophet is in Israel."

When Naaman came to Elisha, he instructed him to wash seven times in the Jordan River, and he did. He became clean. This story has many teaching points: miracles, disobedience/obedience, faith, and mercy. But there's an essential point people often miss. There would be no story had the young, enslaved girl thought of herself as

That Reminds Me of A Story

too small to help. (2 Kings 5)

Julius

Do you realize you can learn much about life from a children's book? For example, a problem can sometimes be kicked back by the person who presented the problem.

I remember a statement in Syd Hoff's "Julius." It is the story of an adolescent boy, Davy, who goes to Africa with his father to catch an animal for the circus.

While looking for a gorilla, Davy found a coconut. He kicked it into the bushes. Someone kicked it back at him! Surprised at this resistance — the coconut being bounced back to him — Davy asks, "Who is in there?" The answer he received was, "I'm a gorilla. My name is Julius."

Sometimes, we kick our problems to God and hope he won't kick them back. We haven't searched out the CAUSE of the problem, WHERE it originated, or some ways to solve it. We don't take any serious action or personal responsibility; we kick the situation to God and hope He doesn't kick it back.

Scripture says that God promised to WORK all things for the good of those who love Him. Notice the word "work" in the previous sentence. We can give our problems (burdens) to God, not because we want to provide God with the problem; we desire to obey the words of Jesus, "Ask, and it will be given to you; seek, and you will find knock, and it will be opened to you. For everyone who asks receives, and the one who seeks finds, and to the one who knocks, it will be opened." (Matthew 7:7-8)

You alone cannot solve all your problems. Only God can. You can give your burdens to the Lord and listen for His directions on how to get involved.

The Greatest Salesman in the World

The motivational speaker said, "Og Mandino wrote and sold over 50 million copies of his books and translated into over 25 languages. It is my opinion," stated the speaker, "Everyone should read his bestselling book 'The Greatest Salesman in the World.'"

The Greatest Salesman in the World tells the story of Hafid, a poor camel boy working for Pathros, a successful trader in Jerusalem. Using the ten scrolls given to him by his master, Pathros, Hafid achieves a life of abundance. Mr. Mandino's book is challenging and will touch your life—for the better.

The speaker declared, "The ten scrolls (principles) to be simple, but not simplistic. They are easy to read, but they can be challenging to adopt. By applying one principle daily, you soon discover your self-image is improving."

Here are ten wisely stated principles of "The Greatest Salesman in the World" by Og Mandino.

1. Today, I have a new life.
2. I will greet each day with love in my heart.
3. I will persist until I succeed.
4. I am nature's greatest miracle.
5. I will live this day as if it is my last.
6. Today, I will master my emotions.
7. I will laugh at the world.
8. Today, I will multiply my value a hundredfold.
9. I will act now.
10. I will pray for guidance.

The Magic of Thinking Big

"Big thinkers train themselves to see not just what is, but what can be." — Dr. David Schwartz.

While in graduate school, I took several marketing courses taught by Dr. David Schwartz, who wrote *The Magic of Thinking Big*. The book has sold over 4 million copies and explains how to set your goals high and exceed them.

In the first class, Dr. Schwartz announced that, although his marketing class did not require purchasing his best-selling book, students who bought the book—specifically the hardback version—usually received higher grades. He stated he would only autograph copies of the hardback version and remember those students as "Big Thinkers." I bought the hard copy, got the autograph, and received A's in both classes.

Dr. Schwartz lectured on teamwork and the need for the team to interact positively to achieve synergy. But his real emphasis and passion were on the individual and their responsibility for their success. The professor believed the words of the Bible when it states, "For as he thinks in his heart, so is he." Swartz taught that you could not inspire the professional without awakening the professional within. What is on the inside shows up on the outside.

In *The Magic of Thinking Big*, Schwartz wrote, "Believe in yourself, and good things happen." His three guides to gaining and strengthening your power of belief are: "1. Think success, don't think failure. At work or in your home, substitute success thinking for failure thinking, and thinking success conditions your mind to create plans that produce success. 2. Remind yourself regularly that you are better than you think. Successful people are ordinary folks who have developed a belief in themselves and what they can do. 3. Believe Big. The size of your belief determines the size of your success. Big ideas and plans are often more straightforward—indeed no more difficult—than small ideas and plans."

"Big thinkers" pay the price for success by pushing themselves beyond what they currently do. Whether in politics, military, business, sports, or any other field, achievers continue to push the envelope. They see limitations as temporary restrictions.

Achievement often requires getting more out of yourself than you've earned. You push yourself beyond your limit and discover you have broken a self-imposing limit.

Roger Bannister broke the racing four-minute mile barrier for the first time on May 6, 1954. Until Bannister ran faster than his "limit," a known scientific "fact," no runner could run a sub-four-minute mile; today, top milers run beyond that barrier; if you want to be a winner and not a loser, you must willingly pay the price by consistently and constantly going or moving beyond your wall.

Sometimes, we are afraid to think big, stand tall, and speak out. I see many people who feel small, slump, and remain mute. These are the people with little goals. Spend little time with these people.

Dr. Schwartz states, "Think little goals "and expect little

achievements. Think big goals and win big success." Perhaps author Claude M. Bristol was right when he wrote, "You have to think big to be big."

Dr. Schwartz signed my copy of his book. "Remember, all things work together for good. So, make good lemonade out of every lemon!"

Take A Message to Garcia and Get it Done

The inspiring story of "A Message to Garcia "is about Colonel Andrew Summers Rowan, a young lieutenant in the United States Army, when the Spanish-American War broke out. President McKinley chose Rowan to deliver a message to General Calixto Garcia, the leader of the revolutionary forces.

Author Elbert Hubbard set the stage for the drama and wrote in his 1899 essay, "Garcia was somewhere in the mountain vastness of Cuba — no one knows where. No mail or telegraph message could reach him. The President must secure his cooperation and quickly."

Lieutenant Rowan held the lowest commission rank in the Army. But having his name suggested to the President, Lieutenant Rowan received the ultimate commendation, "If anybody can find Garcia, it's Rowan."

After receiving his instructions to carry the message to Garcia,

That Reminds Me of A Story

Lieutenant Rowan shook his commander's hand. And without asking one question, he sailed to Cuba with no help or directions other than to deliver the President's message.

With only the help of native guides provided by Cuban patriots, Rowan made his way into the interior mountains and delivered his message to Garcia. The Lieutenant faced many obstacles. As the author of this essay, Elbert Hubbard, writes, "It was the sheer courage and indomitable spirit of the young lieutenant that was at the heart of the accomplishment of his mission."

Elbert Hubbard penned A Message to Garcia over 100 years ago. His book has sold over 40 million copies, and they have translated it into 37 languages, making it one of the highest-selling books in history. Maybe the message of this "old" essay is a new message for change.

How long has it been since your manager gave you an assignment and you took the message to Garcia? Can you remember giving one of your employees a task without questioning what, when, where, why, or how they handled the message to Garcia? When was your last volunteer to take a message to Garcia?

Are you a Rowan? When asked to carry out a task, do you deliver? Do you do more than expected? Are you one of the rare individuals who can take a message to Garcia? Or are you a non-Rowan with a victim mentality, asking many questions and offering many excuses?

SECTION 12:
THE REST OF THE STORIES

That Reminds Me of A Story

Courtesy Is the Minimum for Doing Business

"Give me a stock clerk with a goal, and I'll give you a man who will make history. Give me a man with no goals, and I'll give you a stock clerk." — J.C. Penny.

I recently visited a hardware store to buy a water hose and two water hose connectors. Upon entering, "This is the store with the helpful hardware person," I located a "clerk," who said, "Do you need anything?" Me: "No, I have nothing to do, so I thought I would come in and enjoy your air-conditioned store." That isn't what I said.

I asked for his help to find two water hose couplings. When he showed me two plastic connectors, I said, "I've already tried the cheap ones, and they don't work. I want a better product. At that moment, someone standing behind us interrupted our conversation. He asked, "Do you have anything to eliminate squirrels?" To my surprise, the clerk said, "I don't know, but let's look over here at a couple of aisles." And they walked away.

That didn't seem very smart. I am the current customer. I am spending my money and not looking for a "maybe product." I don't think this clerk remembered the adage, "You dance with the one that brought you."

It makes no difference if you are the customer or the salesperson. Courtesy is the minimum for doing business.

As I left the store, I wondered if I should not have waited for drone delivery at home rather than dealing with the dunce in the aisle. I hope the "friendly place" recognizes that courtesy is the minimum for doing business.

Work in Progress

When I was in school, teachers gave tests; you passed or failed. The bookends of a test were pass A or Fail B. There were markers between B, C, and D, and the report card you carried home reflected these grades (sometimes the teacher added a + or—sign).

Years ago, while walking through my neighborhood, I noticed this message on an elementary school message board, "Students Progress Reports Due This Week." When I was in elementary school, students received "report cards." Now, they call them "progress reports."

There's a big difference between a progress report and a report card. The progress report measures movement toward a goal or goals; a report card reflects degrees of passing or failing. I prefer a progress report.

Do you want to be judged on whether you pass or fail God's service test? Or would you prefer to be graded as a servant in progress?

That Reminds Me of A Story

Life Through the Eyes of a Child

We often think about the good old days and our lives as children. But reality says I am an adult. Paradoxically, people want to be an adult and a child simultaneously. We are always setting out to be a pillar of society and not make a fool of ourselves. But lurking inside of us is a child wanting to get out.

We learn seven critical lessons about life from children.

1. A child is enthusiastic and has boundless energy.
2. A child is a learner.
3. A child quickly forgets and forgives.
4. A child lives in the moment.
5. A child sees beauty in everything.
6. A child colors outside the lines.
7. A child exhibits little prejudice.

I've thought about how nice it would be to be a child again. Whenever this thought comes to mind, my answer is "No!" I have lived in the best times, and I can still improve my life if I only look through a child's eyes.

Keys

Keys. Amazing creations. When there are security considerations, locks can significantly increase the security of your possessions. Many times, the locks require keys.

There are many keys. There are keys to lock and unlock doors, vehicles, mailboxes, travel baggage, and storage locks. Add to that skate, jail cell, or boat key, and you have a lot of different keys.

I have many keys, all without companion lock, stored in a box on my workbench. They are Kwikset, Ace, National Cabinet, Master, Chalet, King Cole, and Sargent, and some are so old that the names aren't readable. They have been around 30—40 years and haven't contributed to anyone's happiness or unhappiness.

Many people have a persistent feeling of ill will or resentment resulting from a past insult or injury locked in their hearts and can't find a key to unlock them. Holding a grudge shows immaturity. It isn't healthy for you and will only create further resentment in your relationship. Love is the key to unlocking a feeling of deep-seated resentment or ill will.

God has strong thoughts about holding grudges. "Do not take revenge or bear a grudge against members of your community but love your neighbor as yourself; I am Yahweh." (Leviticus 19:18, HCSB)

That Reminds Me of A Story

Before deciding what to do with the many keys on my workshop bench, I must use God's love key and unlock my grudges. Someone said holding onto grudges is like swallowing poison and waiting for the other person to die.

Passing on Treasures

I know you didn't ask, but I want to believe my two children would expect me to pass on to them all my treasures: a small bag of 165 colorful marbles from the 40s, primarily top-of-the-line shooters, a slightly used genuine diamond-studied Duncan Yoyo; a Roy Rogers cap pistol with two packages of original caps; a box of never used carbon paper; one each, The Hardy Boys and Nancy Drew books and a genuine railroad spike.

I just remembered a used baseball I bought from a pawnshop in 1948 for twenty-five cents. None of these classic treasures creates ownership excitement with my daughter or son.

I've found satisfaction because I want little, and my needs are provided. None of the items listed are needed, but when I got them, I considered them wants.

Now that I want to pass on these products, no one likes them. Is it possible there's no need for marbles, yoyos, cap guns, and carbon paper? Of all these items, I like marbles the best.

Wayne Nalls

We Work and Often Forget the Reason for the Work

This morning, I encountered an employee who was so focused on doing his job that he missed the reason for his job: satisfying customers.

I went to a grocery store to purchase cream cheese. Because I seldom grocery shop, my wife gave me the in-store location to find the product: "It's on the left wall of the store in the dairy section." The dairy section proved to have more than cream cheese. I found milk, orange juice, butter, eggs, yogurt, but no cream cheese. An employee at the store was replacing cheese in the dairy case. I saw hope and moved beside him. I asked, "Where is the cream cheese?" He continued to restock without looking to his left to see me and remaining bent over. He grunted, "Down there." That was it. I got the message. I was an interruption of his morning and an impediment to accomplishing his job.

I found my cream cheese there and moved to the checkout counter. As I glanced back, the employee was still bent over stocking products—doing his job. He never understood that helping me have a great experience—though it was not written in his employee manual—was his job.

I should have spoken to his manager or even the store manager. My better judgment told me that neither of the managers would use my shopping experience as a teaching moment. Like so many other employees, managers are also working.

When asked why many people fail, the self-made steel tycoon and philanthropist of the 19th century, Andrew Carnegie. He said, "There are two types of people who never achieve much in their lifetimes. One is the person who won't do what they are told to do, and the other is the person who does only what they are told to do."

Often, it is the minor acts that make a big difference. Extra thought, attention, and effort may not change the world, but they can cause someone to feel extraordinary. Today and every day, focus on how to make someone's encounter with you a positive and memorable experience.

The Nearest Exit May Behind You

Merriam-Webster's Collegiate Dictionary defines "Exit" as "the act of going out." That correctly characterizes the innovative organization. Their philosophy is don't look for exit signs. Go out and search for entry signs.

It would be natural to look ahead and not behind. People can't successfully drive a car, peddle a bicycle, or safely walk if they are always looking back. Though it may help to sneak an occasional backward look to ensure your safety, when it comes to achievement, the past is just that, the past. Former professional baseball pitcher and Hall of Famer Leroy Robert "Satchel" Paige said, "Don't look back — something might be gaining on you."

On a flight out of Tampa, Florida, I listened—a good idea— to the flight attendant's mandatory preflight safety announcements. She addressed seat belts, oxygen masks, no smoking, float devices, service trays, etc. When she talked about exiting the plane, she told us to look at the closest exit sign should an emergency occur. And the flight attendant reminded the passengers that the nearest exit might be behind, even in the next row back.

A quick look back helps an organization realize whether it is on target or missing the goal. Are sales on target? Is employee morale high or improving? Are customers delighted with your service? Is your market share increasing, decreasing, or stagnant? What is your ROI? Is the organization innovating as it should? You are achieving your goals, or you are not. Recognize the shortfalls and take corrective action. Tout the achievements and build on the momentum. Look back and verify that the objectives you set in the past are still realistic.

The past is often a burden for the future. Even when executed brilliantly today, a strategy that produced success in the past frequently leads to failure. Blame it on change. Great advertising executive Bruce Barton observed, "When you are through changing, you are through." Look at a caterpillar and look at a butterfly. The only connection is change. As someone has said, "If nothing ever changed, there'd be no butterflies." While what's behind (the past) is essential, it is also necessary to look around (the present). Both the past and the present are often harbingers of the future. A sensitive appraisal of today, viewed in the light of history, can help eliminate repeating historical mistakes. With the future just ahead, don't get caught looking back.

Two Perspectives

During my sophomore and junior high school years, I picked watermelons in the fields and packed them into semi-trailers. It was hard work and long days. We started at 6:00 a.m. and finished at 7:30 p.m. The field temperature was in the 60s early morning and rose to 100 degrees by 2:00 p.m.

The watermelon farmer paid me one dollar per hour, including lunch. Most times, the farmer received one dollar per melon shipped. I had no problem with the financial arrangement. After all, the farmer was an entrepreneur who owned the land and paid for the seeds, fertilizer, planting costs, shipping costs, and harvesting costs.

My problem was the length of the long rows. Those seemingly unending rows that disappeared in the distance were demoralizing. Why couldn't the farmer plant shorter melon rows and give me a sense of accomplishment? I could quickly work a row with shorter rows and then be in the next row. This action would provide a psychological momentum and a sense of accomplishment.

The farmer was interested in productivity and maximizing the use of his land. The long rows secured that goal.

Life is like a watermelon row, a long journey. Often, I wish I could see the end of the trip, be refreshed with minor victories, and not have so many deferred accomplishments.

The Obvious Case for a Garage

We have more stored junk in the United States than people in most countries even have.

At a recently conducted garage sale, one buyer commented, "There's so much stuff in there." When was the last time your car was in it?" I answered, "Never. I have lived here for fourteen years, and my car has never been inside the garage." Here are a few homes with garage stats you might relate to - 24% of homeowners are embarrassed to leave their garage doors open. (Impulse Research survey) - 66% of all occupied housing units in the United States had a garage or carport. (U.S. Bureau of the Census 2017 American Housing Survey)

That Reminds Me of A Story

A survey of realtors reveals that garages ranked higher as desirable storage spaces for homebuyers than basements or attics. Twenty percent of Garage Living poll respondents said they could not park in their garage.

In a U.S. Department of Energy study, 50% of homeowners named the garage the most cluttered and disorganized area of their house. 25% of people with 2-car garages don't park in them, and a third can only park one car because of garage clutter.

Rentable storage space is another way to protect, shelter, or store our goods. About 9% of Americans rent storage space, even though 65% of those homeowners have a garage. (Self-Storage Association stat). They estimate 45,000-60,000 shelf-storage units in America with over 1.7 billion square feet of storage capacity. I have 10x20-ft storage space and a two-car garage. In the garage, I have about $1,500 of junk. My $35,000 automobile weathers outside.

Should Company Restroom Expenses be Included in the Marketing Budget?

Businesses spend billions each year on marketing to draw in customers. The strategy attempts to put the company's best foot forward to win business. TV and radio commercials, print ads, web advertising, etc., try to build a positive relationship with customers and prospects. Too often, employees at the customer's physical contact point undermine this strategic communication effort.

Four Negative Physical Customer Contact Points 1. Incompetent and unconcerned employees 2. Unfriendly customer policies, rules, and procedures 3. Inferior products or services 4. Faulty or unclean company restrooms

I take it for granted that the first three of the four negative customer physical constant points need no further explanation. But item four, "faulty or unclean restrooms," may require some proof.

You say, "A restroom is a restroom." I contend you responded too quickly if you believe that statement. As we go about our lives, we experience four classifications of company restrooms: I. The 4-Star, top-of-the-line bathroom, 2. The 2-star, adequate toilet, 3. They let me get in and out of the restroom, and 4—the restroom from hell. From personal experience, I believe the total number of bathrooms in this classification is in reverse order, with number 4 being the most prevalent, number three being the next most experienced restroom, and so on.

A friend shared two statements from a speech he recently heard. The CEO speaker stated he had only two company rules. First, employees must treat every other person in the enterprise like family. Second, are you ready for this? They must keep all company bathrooms in a 4-star condition. He explained that he is adamant about this rule because the cleanliness of the company restrooms reflects how the company treats its "family." Think about that for a moment.

When my wife and I travel north on I-75, we stop in Tifton, GA, at Adcock's Pecans. This store features great pecans, jellies, and candies. But we stopped because my wife believes Adcock's has the cleanest restrooms of any business along I-75. She enthusiastically passes this information to many of our friends for their north travel. We stopped for the restrooms and made our purchases, feeling sure that our products would also be good with clean bathrooms.

Someone said, "Cleanliness is next to godliness," but do businesses understand that a clean restroom is close to their customer's pocketbooks? Dirty bathrooms, uncaring people, poor policies, and inferior products and services drive customers from the business. Spotless, hygienic, clean restrooms help build successful organizations, sell products, and create powerful word-of-mouth advertising. What do your company restrooms say about you?

Don't Be Fooled by the Mask

Many people, hoping to avoid being the next COVID case, wear masks, practice social distancing, and wash their hands. I practice all three.

Wayne Nalls

As a mask user, I wanted to know more about its safety. I read an article in Wired Magazine about using light and candle tests to check for a mask's efficiency: "A mask's weave should be tight enough not to allow light to show through and thick enough to prevent you from blowing out a candle while you're wearing it." Masks are designed to protect you from infecting someone else or affecting you.

People use masks to cover up something. A bank robber uses his mask to cover up his identity. In ancient Greece, stage actors used masks to pretend to be someone else.

We get the word hypocrite from the Greek word "hypokrites", which means "pretender". A hypocrite is a person who pretends to be a certain way but acts and believes the total opposite. Even a person who washes their hands, stands six feet away, and wears a mask can still be a hypocrite.

Some people pretend to be friends to your face, and they speak ill of you behind your back. Be wary of the "stage actor" or pretender who shows affection but is jealous and filled with envy. Don't be fooled by the person who wears a mask. The only person to wear a mask and remain the same person with or without the mask was The Lone Ranger.

That Reminds Me of A Story

What Has Society Done That David Copperfield Couldn't?

"The real secret of magic lies in the performance." — David Copperfield

Pulling the rabbit out of a hat is elementary. Walking through the Great Wall of China and making The Statue of Liberty disappear is illusion artistry. But legendary American illusionist David Copperfield did both. According to Forbes magazine, making things vanish makes Copperfield the most commercially successful magician in history.

But society accomplished what even David Copperfield couldn't. Many people (societies' illusionary magicians) made two former honorable words — "responsibility" and "accountability"— disappear from daily use. The words are synonyms; they have the same or nearly the same meaning. The two terms are in a current dictionary but have disappeared from personal and professional life.

Is it only an illusion? Find an employee (including supervisors, managers, and owners) who accepts ownership of a problem, initiative, timeline, or project outcome. Instead of being responsible and accountable, many people use the antonym victim to describe how they are affected by forces beyond their control.

Even the team concept encourages the illusion. The team is responsible and accountable, but not the individual. The buck stops with the team but not at an individual's desk.

Hiring, training, and promoting people who accept responsibility and are accountable are requisites for any successful organization. Leaders know keenly that their organizations need people who take ownership of a problem or project or turn a prospect into a satisfied customer. These "magic" makers pull success out of a hat. They want the ball, the last at-bat, the last shot, and one more minute. These magic makers crave the responsibility for selling tickets, packing stadiums, filling theaters, and putting dollars to the bottom line.

Profitable organizations correlate the number of accountable and responsible employees with the likelihood of continued success. These employees are also recognized and rewarded accordingly.

The word "we" is an inclusive term often used to denote a team and share recognition and reward. We encourage people not to utilize "I" as it sounds like one person takes credit for the outcome. I agree with the logic, but sometimes, "I" is appropriate. One of those occasions is when I accept responsibility or am accountable.

We have words like self-improvement, self-discipline, and self-image. I wish more people would add self-responsibility and self-accountability to their vocabulary.

There are several ways to end this story. I chose a quote from a

That Reminds Me of A Story

highly successful magician in history: "I try to help people realize their dreams by using magic to tell stories that educate, move, and inspire."

Don't be Disqualified for the Trophy

They say that winning the Super Bowl Trophy is priceless. Well, that's not entirely accurate. The Super Bowl Trophy costs $50,000 and requires four months and 72 hours of labor. Crafted entirely of sterling silver by Tiffany & Co. silversmiths, it stands 22 inches high and weighs 7 lbs.

Please indulge me while I think about another trophy: my trophy. It is 11 inches high and weighs 1 pound. The plaque reads "Wayne Nalls Most Valuable Back Ocala High School 1957".

The trophy symbolizes anything taken in competition, especially when preserved as an award, and is evidence of victory, valor, skill, etc.

The oldest sports trophies in the world are the Carlisle Bells, a horse racing trophy dating back to 1559 and 1599. But the Apostle captured the spirit of a Christian's award in 1 Corinthians 9:24-27. "Do you not know that all the runners run in a race, but only one gets the prize? Run in such a way as to get the prize. Everyone who competes in the games goes into strict training. They do it to get a crown that will not last, but we get one that will last forever. Therefore, I do not run like a man running aimlessly; I do not fight like a man beating the air. No, I beat my body and make it my slave so that after I have preached to others, I will not be disqualified for the prize."

Winning the Super Bowl Trophy or receiving a personal trophy on your desk pales compared to the heavenly award that lasts forever.

Maps and Directions

I love maps and can't follow directions. My wife doesn't need a map or directions. Once she has been somewhere, she can return to that location without help. (Like a homing pigeon or a monarch butterfly returning from the US and Canada, where they breed, and hibernate in central Mexico, where they).

I used to collect highway maps. As I crossed into a new state, I got them from gas stations and state welcome centers. My favorite place was Cracker Barrel; I picked up a United States map showing their locations and could have an excellent meal while in the restaurant. After I got married, my wife and I joined AAA and used their great travel maps.

When I pull into a gas station (no longer called a service station), I never ask for a map. They no longer have one. And the person inside

That Reminds Me of A Story

the store doesn't know how to get from his location to anywhere else, including destinations in his hometown. And indeed, don't ask for local restaurant recommendations.

They depicted ancient forms of maps on clay tablets and cave walls. Today, maps are readily available on cell phones, wristwatches, car monitors, computers, and other electronic tracking devices. Map production has come a long way, but I still need help following directions.

Corrugated Cardboard Boxes

I have two cardboard boxes sitting next to my desk in my bedroom. A visitor would say they looked out of place.

One box is six by nine inches, and the other is 8x11. What are three interesting facts about cardboard? The smaller box easily fits into the larger one. The boxes protect something from Amazon Prime. Printed on each side of the boxes are the words, "This box is now made with less material." Less weight is the manufacturer's goal. The soaring cost of transportation is another factor.

Since American printer Robert Gair produced the first efficient cardboard box in 1879, people have found thousands of uses for cardboard. With the increase in production, the United States uses over 80 billion corrugated boxes annually. Recycling one ton of cardboard can save over nine cubic yards of landfill space.

Wayne Nalls

Manufacturers package about 80% of products sold in the United States in cardboard. I'm saving the two boxes next to my desk to store everyday life stuff. Stuff I do not need today.

That Reminds Me of A Story

SECTION 13:
STORIES TO BRIGHTEN YOUR DAY
Down to Earth stories With Up to Heaven Truths

Twinkling of an Eye

Someone characterized the "twinkling of the eye" as the time it takes for light to enter, reach the back of the eye, and be reflected out. Light travels at 186,000 miles per second, so the Twinkle is about one billionth of a second. That's fast!

I am reminded of three examples of the use of "twinkle."

The first example is from one of the most beloved nursery lullaby songs, "Twinkle, Twinkle, Little Star." The second example comes from "The Night Before Christmas." "So up to the house-top the coursers they flew, with the sleigh full of toys, and St. Nicholas too. And then, in a twinkle, I heard the prancing and pawing of each little hoof on the roof.

The Bible provides the third example. In 1 Corinthians 15:51- 52, St. Paul writes, "Behold, I tell you a mystery; we will not all sleep, but we will all be changed, in a moment, in the twinkling of an eye, at the last trumpet; for the trumpet will sound, and the dead will be raised imperishable, and we will be changed."

When Jesus returns, it's over. He appears in a twinkle of the eye. In about one billionth of a second, your everlasting life is determined. He will define your destination. If Jesus is your Savior and Lord, He will take you to Heaven. When the trumpet sounds and the shout from the archangel is heard, Jesus will take those who have accepted

Him as their Savior and Lord to Heaven. It will be too late to surrender your life to the Lord. You have a twinkling of the eye moment. And it will be over before you even realize you are exiled from God forever. A time without end!

The Salty, Savory Sea

I was desperate for water as I sat in the First Baptist Church of Merritt Island, Florida.

Yet, 60 years later, I remember the sermon. I sat spelled bound, listening to Dr. Adrian Rogers preach an incredible sermon. I still recall its title, "The Salty Savory Sea." Dr. Rogers' sermon was based on the apostle Paul's voyage, recorded in Acts 27.

Around 60 A.D., a ship carrying the apostle Paul and 276 men plus grain cargo shipwrecked off Malta's coast. They were taking Paul to Rome to be tried as a political rebel.

Scripture says the ship was caught in a violent storm during this ill-fated first-century journey to Rome. The crew jettisoned the ship's tackle and cargo, released the lifeboat, and even passed ropes under the ship to hold it together. After 14 days of weather so severe that neither the sun nor stars were visible, all seemed lost.

As Dr. Rogers spoke about the crew jettisoning all the cargo, he emphasized the pounding of the salty, savory sea. My mouth became dryer and dryer — I needed a glass of water.

God sent Paul encouragement and promised that everyone on the ship would survive. God understands our fear. We may feel anxious and afraid of our storms, but if we look to God, He will strengthen and encourage us.

We can't always predict life's storms. But storms will come. Often, we create our storms by making wrong decisions, and sometimes, the storms result from unknown factors. You may have to jettison your baggage.

Whenever I see the words "Sea Salt," I need water.

A Story of Two Donkeys

I read that the donkey dates back 3,000 years before the birth of Jesus. Although serving as a lowly beast of burden, the donkey served Mary and her son, Jesus. When we explore Jesus' life, we discover the story of two donkeys. Each had a significant role in Jesus' life. The two donkeys are aptly named "Privilege" and "Honor. "

"Privilege" had a vital transportation role. Christians believe Mary rode a donkey from Nazareth to Bethlehem just before the birth of

That Reminds Me of A Story

Jesus. The Scriptures do not expressly state that she did; however, it is doubtful that Mary, who was in such an advanced pregnancy, walked from Nazareth to Bethlehem, about 90 miles. The grueling trip and stressful environment may have taken them four to seven days. They entrusted "Privilege" to carry the pregnant Mary.

Thirty-three years later, Jesus rode the donkey "Honor" into Jerusalem to fulfill the prophecy. The Old Testament prophet Zechariah, writing in 484 B.C., noted, "Rejoice greatly, O daughter of Zion! Shout in triumph, O daughter of Jerusalem! Behold, your king is coming to you; He is just and endowed with salvation, Humble, and mounted on a donkey, even on a colt, the foal of a donkey." (Zechariah 9:9)

The Apostle Matthew adds, "Tell Daughter Zion, look, your King is coming to you, gentle, and mounted on a donkey, even on a colt, the foal of a beast of burden." (Matthew 21:5, HCSB)

I believe that "Privilege" and "Honor" teach us it's an honor to transport the Gospel and a privilege to share the Good News with humility.

The Bible's First Ventriloquist

As a kid, I ordered a ventriloquist kit advertised on the back of a comic book. Two weeks later, it arrived. I skimmed the directions.

"Place the small item in the back of the throat and exert pressure on it by placing the tongue on the front of the upper front teeth." I did so and almost suffocated before getting the item out of my throat. I didn't need the dummy to talk to me. The dummy was me.

Edgar Bergen, Terry Fator, and Darci Lynne Farmer are well-known ventriloquists.

We consider Fred Russell the father of modern ventriloquism, but the evidence dates to ancient Egypt. But the Hebrew Bible has an earlier narrative of ventriloquism. Moses first used ventriloquism in ancient biblical times during the Exodus.

Exodus chapter 4 contains the story of God sending Moses back to Egypt with the message to let His people go. But Moses said to the LORD, "Oh, my Lord, I am not eloquent, either in the past or since you have spoken to your servant, but I am slow of speech and of the tongue. 'Please, Lord, send someone else.' "Then the Lord's anger burned against Moses, and He said, 'Isn't Aaron the Levite, your brother? I know he can speak well.'"

God instructed Moses to speak with his brother and put the words into his mouth, "He shall speak for you to the people, and he shall be your mouth, and you shall be as God to him."

There you have it. Moses was the first ventriloquist.

That Reminds Me of A Story

I Did Not See That Coming

Looking forward to an excellent breakfast is one of the pleasures of life, and my wife and I ate breakfast at Bob Evans this morning. We went to Denny's, but the wait for food was 45 minutes. Customers weren't the problem; the issue was preparing the meals. When told of the delay, we went next door to Bob Evans.

I told my wife, "Three pancakes are too many as we ate. The restaurant could serve two pancakes at the same price, and no one would complain." She agreed.

Later, when the server brought our bill, I commented to her about my suggestion of one less pancake. She said, "You're right; many customers tell me that. But some couples serve the third pancake to one of their young children, and along with juice, it's the child's breakfast.

I did not see that coming.

Sundays, I see people arriving late for worship. Don't they know to be on time? Don't they realize they are disrupting the service? Some leave before they complete the service. Aren't they aware the service has led to this spiritual point, and another member in the congregation may make a significant life-changing decision?

Suppose a person gets up in the morning, feels terrible, and runs late. They could decide not to attend because they are already late.

Something inside them says, "Go anyway." A young couple's child is dressed and ready; then they throw up. Do the parents clean up the child and arrive late? Or do they say, "It is not our day; we'll go next Sunday?"

The person who arrives late or leaves early may have a legitimate reason. Why don't I pass on judging and keep focused on the message in the sermon for me?

I did not see that coming.

Disciple May Describe It Best

Several months ago, my wife and I bought an iPad at Best Buy. We quickly found that customer service people are hard to locate, and knowledgeable ones are even more difficult to identify. But we encountered a family of four waiting for anyone to help them.

I don't know whether it's me or life, but I seldom strike up conservation without reason with strangers. But I felt urged to ask the father if he was a Christian. He said, "Don't get me wrong, but I don't identify as a Christian. I prefer to say I am a disciple. Many people say they are Christian, but their actions prove otherwise."

When I got home, I researched the concept of discipleship. The dictionary on my computer defines "discipleship as the condition or situation of being a disciple, a follower, or a student of some philosophy, especially a follower of Christ."

The father I talked with is correct. Christian discipleship means more than church membership, Bible reading, and praying. It signifies a relationship with the master teacher, following Him, and imitating His way of life. His teaching shapes your life.

The Nursery Mom

She wasn't a pastor, deacon, or church staff member. She didn't teach a Sunday School class or oversee a church committee. She didn't attend Sunday School or the morning worship service. But she was the queen of the church nursery.

All the church congregation — young and old — knew Mrs. Harward. During her thirty years of queenship, she changed the diapers of many of the congregation's young adults and teenage members.

I remember Mrs. Hardward as faithful: she was on deck every Sunday. She loved the children and their parents, and the parents and children responded with love for her. She had the patience of a saint with so many diapers to change. She produced the fruits of the Holy Spirit in her life and fulfilled her purpose by living out the scripture verse, "Whatsoever the hand finds to do, do it."

The day God called the "Nursery Mom" home, He welcomed her with these words, "Welcome home, thy good and faithful servant, and I want you to meet Dorcas.

Don't Look for Level Plains. Climb Mountains

"Our lives should have depth, which means pushing ourselves out of our comfort zones and not taking the easy way out all the time." Author: Marie Tillman

There is no easy way to go from the plain to the mountaintop, and no one has developed a three-step program for summiting. People often seek the easy way and hope to avoid life's obstacles, but the obstacles are there to make you a more vigorous climber.

Walking on the plains is easy. Climbing mountains is difficult. Climbing tall mountains is almost impossible. Don't Look for Level Plains. Climb mountains with practice and determination; you can climb further each day. Welcome the struggle. Accept the challenge. Stay Focused. Climb your mountain. There's never anything to be gained by walking the plains. Don't be guilty of taking the simple path.

The Old Testament hero, Caleb, at 85, showed resolve in his request to Joshua, "Now, therefore, give me this mountain, of which the Lord spake in that day; for thou heardest in that day how the

That Reminds Me of A Story

Anakims were there, and that the cities were great and fenced: if so be the Lord will be with me, then I shall be able to drive them out, as the Lord said." (Joshua 14:12)

Straddling your mountain with one foot in Heaven and the other on Earth, you see clearly that the climb was worth it.

When the Gospel Songs Go Silent

Growing up in a Southern Baptist church, I heard many Gospel songs you seldom hear today. These are excellent songs with a timeless message.

Recently, I attended an outdoor memorial service for a relative of my wife. They conducted the service in a farming community on a beautiful hill outside Dade City, Florida.

There were more than 100 family attendees — three daughters and their husbands, another daughter and a son and his wife. Then, there were the kids' grandkids and great-grandkids. Plus, I have many close friends.

We were seated beneath six Old Florida oak trees that provided shade and a remarkable backdrop for the service on chairs. The service featured Aunt Charlotte's favorite gospel songs: "Sweet Holy Spirit," "What a Friend We Have in Jesus," "Morning Has

Broken," "I Believe," and "Going Home."

These songs, long silent in churches, now provided a voice and a message that God still reigns and cares for His own. Aunt Charlotte is one of His own and currently sings in the huge Heavenly choir.

Sadly, it took a family homecoming to revive the old gospel songs. I wish the music had lasted longer so that I could reminisce about the early church where I first heard them.

Journey to the Top

Climbing the world's tallest mountains presents both extreme physical and mental challenges.

In 1997, Jon Krakauer published Into Thin Air. He wrote about his Mount Everest experience when eight climbers died after getting trapped in an unexpected storm. People magazine described the book as "a harrowing tale of the perils of high-altitude climbing, a story of terrible luck, worst judgment, and heartbreaking heroism."

While Mount Everest is almost five times higher than Mount Sinai, Scripture speaks of the perils of high-altitude climbing on Mount Sinai. Moses led the people out of Egypt, and God came down to the top of Mount Sinai and invited Moses to meet Him. At their summit meeting, God gave Moses the Ten Commandments for

That Reminds Me of A Story

living a life pleasing to Him.

In Deuteronomy, chapters 19:18- 20, we read: "Mount Sinai was covered with smoke because the Lord descended on it in fire. The smoke billowed up from it like smoke from a furnace, and the whole mountain trembled violently. The Lord descended to the top of Mount Sinai and called Moses to the top of the mountain. So, Moses went up."

Krakauer climbed his mountain. And Moses climbed his mountain. God presents all Christians with their mountain. Can you say with Caleb (an Old Testament climber), "Give me my mountain. I'm prepared to climb?"

A Two-Part Command: Ask and Seek

A friend told me about a young Army Captain who had been a POW during the Vietnam conflict. Captain Burns had spoken to his Kiwanis Club. And he said the captain's speech was an excellent and moving personal testimony about God's grace.

I was the Church Training Director for the Riverside Baptist Church in Tampa, Florida. Because evening attendance was declining, I created a promotional program called "Evening of Encounter." Our goal was 200 people, but our average attendance was around 75.

Friends helped promote the program.

We invited Captain Burns and set a date and attendance goal for 200 people.

On May 5, 1974, our church met to hear Captain Burns. After his excellent presentation, we counted the size of the audience: 199 people. We asked for 200 people and were one short of the goal.

Hadn't Jesus said, "Ask, and it will be given to you; seek, and you will find; knock, and the door will be opened to you. For everyone who asks receives; the one who seeks finds; and to the one who knocks, the door will be opened." (Matthew 7:7-8, NIV)

Looking in the second row was a tiny baby we overlooked. We received what we had asked for 200 people in attendance. But only after we followed the second part of Jesus' promise, "Seek, and you will find."

That's Not What We Do Here

A friend shared her family's experience searching for a new church home. She, her husband, and a 12-year-old daughter visited a local church and had this experience. No one introduced themselves or asked if they were visitors. After requesting directions, someone told them where to go, but no one accompanied them.

That Reminds Me of A Story

The pastor asked everyone to stand and shake hands with the person next to them during the service. This copout is a poor example of a "friendly church." After the service, no one spoke to them, thanked them for attending; no one said, "Hope to see you next Sunday."

This church missed an opportunity to build relationships with a young couple and their daughter. They lost the chance to make sure the family knew Jesus. Before you skip another event, ensure all members understand the priority of relationship building, and anyone with the slightest chance of encountering a "visitor" starts the relationship building.

In saying, "That's not what we do here," the church didn't step outside the box and missed out on new members, tithers, workers, and the blessed opportunity to help mold a young girl's Christian life.

We must focus on the problems we can solve. The problem is that no one cared. When we love one another as Christ loves us, the problem disappears.

Diamonds are Forever

Do you know the two most prominently selling diamond engagement rings? Number one is the solitaire ring. The gemstone is set high, allowing maximum diamond exposure to light and enhancing its brilliance.

The second best-selling engagement is the Halo. This "ethereal" style ring has a central gemstone surrounded by a "halo" of smaller diamonds to emphasize its sparkle and make it appear larger. The stones in both types of rings are scarce. Because they are rare, diamonds are among the most valuable substances on Earth. Besides its trademark brilliance and fire, the diamond's strength and durability are predominant traits. It's the hardest mineral known to man, making it a prime substance for cutting and drilling.

Engineers developed a synthetic diamond. These lab-grown rocks look genuine, but these synthetic diamonds don't have the same properties as natural diamonds.

Satan attempts to be a synthetic god and woo us in his ways, but he doesn't have the same properties as God. God's love lasts forever. The guarantees and durability of this bond guarantee you a home in heaven.

It is no mistake that most weddings worldwide — celebrity or not— involve a sparkling diamond. Diamonds are rare, and they are forever. God's love is inexhaustible and eternal.

As God created the diamond, He wonderfully made you a sparkling, beautiful, and exceptional person.

That Reminds Me of A Story

Kindness

People expect kindness from their families and friends. We also express empathy toward others we know.

But what happens when we are kind to people we don't know? And what are the results when people we don't understand show us kindness?

Many people are guilty of not showing compassion for strangers. Demonstrating kindness to people we don't know requires stepping outside the box and engaging in the unfamiliar: people, needs, circumstances, language, skin color, and new ideas.

In Ephesians 4:32, Paul instructs Christians to "be kind to another, tenderhearted, forgiving one another, even as God for Christ's sake hath forgiven you."

When a stranger shows kindness toward us, our initial reaction is shock, embarrassment, and bewilderment. Our first question is, "Why is the individual doing this for me?" Don't be ungrateful or unappreciative. Being a cheerful and thankful receiver is essential. Allow the other to give you something, even if it is a kind word.

What if we could understand the roots of kindness — and accept a fundamental principle of life that we have just received a gift from God by being thankful for a deed of kindness? In being grateful, we show appreciation for God's blessing.

Wayne Nalls

Never underestimate the power of kindness.

Prayer Is Talking with God

There have always been stories of prayer because that is how we talk to God. Of all the prayers, the most famous is The Lord's Prayer. Jesus taught His disciples how they should pray. Beginning with, "Our Father in heaven, hallowed be your name." (Matthew 6:9).

The second best-known prayer is The Prayer of Jabez. A book about it was published in 2000; it has sold over nine million copies and became an international bestseller, topping the New York Times bestseller list. One reason for the book's success is one verse in the Old Testament, gives four essential points on how a godly man should pray.

The prayer is simple: "And Jabez called on the God of Israel saying, 'Oh, that You would bless me indeed, and enlarge my territory, that Your hand would be with me, and that You would keep me from evil, that I may not cause pain. So, God granted him what he requested." (1 Chronicles 4:10, HCSB)

We remember Jabez for his prayer rather than a heroic act. He asks God to.

- Bless Him.

- Help enlarge his territory (center of influence).
- Be with him in all he did.
- Keep him from evil and harm.

Are you an honorable man or woman like Jabez? Use these four simple keys to guide your prayer life. Ask God to bless you, enlarge your influence, put His hand on you, and keep you from evil.

As with Jabez, God will answer your prayer.

Zippo Lighter

You can buy a Zippo lighter from Walmart, Amazon, and many other outlets, as well as at garage sales. At one of my garage sales, a buyer asked if I had any old cigarette lighters. No, but I have one stored away somewhere.

I had put it away somewhere, but where?

After a week of searching, I found the Zippo in a shoebox in the back of my rented storage locker. Though over 50 years old, the lighter still looks new. I don't know where it came from or the original owner's name.

The company has produced over 400,000,000 Zippo lighters since 1933. The lighter quickly became prominent during World War II.

The Guinness Book of World Records estimated that over 5 billion copies of the Bible are in print.

While Christians are not to be compared to Zippo lighters, they are to be light. Jesus said to his followers, "You are the light of the world. A town built on a hill cannot be hidden. Neither do people light a lamp and put it under a bowl. Instead, they put it on its stand, and it gives light to everyone in the house." (Matthew 5:14,15, HCBS)

The Zippo lighter has one easily recognized sound — it clicks. The Bible has one easily recognized voice—God's.

People Can Put You in a Pit

The Bible describes a pit as a place where demons are imprisoned. Christians see it as a place of unresolved problems, despair, discouragement, depression, and abandonment.

Scripture gives two excellent examples of God lifting two righteous men from their pit: Joseph and Jeremiah. Joseph, one of the biblical patriarch Jacob's twelve sons, was thrown into a pit by his brothers, who resented their father's favoritism towards him. Although they later sold him into slavery. He rose to become master of Egypt.

The prophet Jeremiah was dropped into a pit at King Zedekiah's

That Reminds Me of A Story

command. He had angered the king by saying Jerusalem would fall to the king of Babylon. Which soon happened.

Using Jeremiah's friend, Ebed-Melech, God took men with him and went to the pit. He brought some old rags and worn-out clothes and let them down with ropes to Jeremiah in the pit, and they pulled him up with the ropes and lifted him out of the pit.

Trust God to transform your discouragement into peace and your despair into triumph. Consider a few life lessons to be learned from the pit.

1. Ask yourself, "Why am I in the pit?"
2. What can I do to get out of the pit?
3. Pray for God's deliverance from the pit.
4. Praise God for lifting you out of the pit.
5. Learn from mistakes.
6. Forgive yourself. Everyone makes mistakes.
7. The former problem into an opportunity.

When you've fallen into a pit, the thing you need most to escape is not a ladder. You need an intense longing for God to bring you up from the pit. People can place you in a pit, and people can also lift you out. In the pit, there is only one direction to look up. In the storms of life, there is only one direction to look: up to God.

Meditation

What does it mean for Christians to meditate? The Bible suggests we do more than just read it; we think, reflect, contemplate, and let its truths guide our actions. According to God, He says this about meditation.

"Blessed is the one who does not walk in step with the wicked or stand in the way that sinners take or sit in the company of mockers, but whose delight is in the law of the Lord, and who meditates on his law day and night." (Psalms 1 and 2)

"This Book of the Law shall not depart from your mouth, but you shall meditate on it day and night, so that you may be careful to do according to all that is written in it. For then you will make your way prosperous, and then you will have good success." (Joshua 1:8)

The secret to happiness may be a time of meditation each day. Here's a simple step-by-step guide to help you meditate on God's word daily.

1. Choose a time and place to meditate on the Word of God.

2. Pray for understanding.

3. Pick a chapter. Read each verse slowly.

4. What stands out?

5. Write your thoughts down.

6. Determine how to apply these thoughts in your life.

The key to success is reflecting on the Bible and carefully following what you read. Marcus Aurelius is quoted as having said, "Dwell on the beauty of life. Watch the stars and see yourself running with them ... The happiness of your life depends upon the quality of your thoughts (meditations)."

Daily Affirmation: I can meditate on my life's purpose in everything I do.

The Blue Cow

Driving through the countryside, seeing a blue cow eating green grass and producing white milk would be strange. It is improbable that you will notice a blue cow. But if you do, the sighting would be remarkable.

The Bible tells a story about a blue cow named Lazarus who lived, died, and was resurrected. Lazarus and his two sisters, Mary and Martha, were close friends of Jesus, who previously had been a guest in their home.

When notified of Lazarus's severe health problem, Jesus told His disciples, "Lazarus, our friend, has just fallen asleep. It's time that I go and awaken him." When they heard this, the disciples replied, "Lord, if he has just fallen asleep, he'll get better." Jesus spoke about the death of Lazarus, but the disciples presumed he was talking about natural sleep. Then Jesus made it plain to them, "Lazarus is dead." (John 11:14)

When Jesus and the disciples arrived, people told Him that Lazarus was dead, but if he had come earlier, Jesus would have healed him. But that would not be a blue cow. Jesus did the remarkable and raised Lazarus from the dead.

We didn't see a blue cow today because our eyes were closed. We must ask God to open them to see the improbable, the blue cow. In the book of Kings (2 Kings 6), the Bible describes how God answered Elisha's prayer and opened his servant's eyes so that he could see the angelic army leading horses and chariots of fire surrounding and protecting them.

Sometimes, you find blue cows in places you least expect. You see them in a burning bush, a talking donkey, a fiery chariot, and a no-name good Samaritan. Blue cows reveal what we consider improbable, yet God reveals it as possible.

That Reminds Me of A Story

The Unsung Man of Trust

Each time I pass by a homeless person, I am reminded of the story of the Good Samaritan recorded in Luke 10:25- 37. The passage speaks of at least six people: the traveler victim, the Good Samaritan, thieves, a Priest, a Levite, and the nameless innkeeper. It is the often-overlooked innkeeper who teaches us lessons we need to know.

I know you are familiar with the story, but have you identified yourself with one of the six people mentioned in Jesus' parable? If so, which one?

The Parable of the Good Samaritan tells the story of a Jewish man traveling from Jerusalem to Jericho. This winding 8-mile downhill road was a favorite hideout of robbers and thieves. And while on the way, he is beaten by thieves and robbed of everything he has.

But a Samaritan on his journey came upon him. And when he saw the victim, he had compassion. He went over to him and bandaged his wounds, pouring on olive oil and wine. Then, he put the man on his animal, brought him to an inn, and cared for him. The next day, he took out two denarii, gave them to the innkeeper, and said, "Take care of him. When I return, I'll reimburse you for whatever extra expenses you incur."

Though the parable focuses on The Good Samaritan, the story

includes the innkeeper and his trust that The Good Samaritan would return and pay for the extra expense. The often-overlooked innkeeper teaches us a lesson about faith and hospitality. The unknown innkeeper trusted the Good Samarian to settle the bills for the beaten and bleeding traveler left in his care. He also had to help to provide first aid to the traveler.

Jesus tells us to follow the Samaritan's example to inherit eternal life. We are to "Love the Lord your God with all your heart, with all your soul, with all your strength, and with all your mind; and your neighbor as yourself." We need to show compassion and love for those we encounter in our everyday activities.

Every day, we pass by people who need our help, encouragement, foodstuff, and shelter. Do you identify as the traveler victim, the Good Samaritan, the thieves, the Priest, the Levite, or the nameless innkeeper?

About the Author

Wayne Nalls is a Student of Continuous Learning, Author, Workshop Leader, and Speaker who finds magic in people's personal stories.

Made in United States
Orlando, FL
25 July 2024